ON THE STARTING

A HISTORY OF ATHLETICS IN LEICESTER

BY JIM SHARLOTT

FOREWORD BY SEBASTIAN COE

INCLUDING ILLUSTRATIONS BY
GEORGE HERRINGSHAW

CONTENTS

ACKNOWLEDGEMENTS

I am grateful to all those individuals and organisations who have provided me with practical help and encouragement in the course of researching and writing this book. City stalwarts Stan Dawson, Life Vice President of the County AAA, and George White, President of the English Cross Country Union, drew on their deep experience of the local scene. The late Reg Burton, former County Schools AA Secretary, and Arthur Capers, retired Head of Enderby C of E School, lucidly uncovered pointers to early schools history; and Albert Johnson of Leicester Walking Club provided invaluable insights into race walking in Leicester. Immense help was provided at the National Centre of Athletics Literature at Birmingham University by John Bromhead of Oakham School, whose 1972 catalogue of the Centre's contents has illuminated many research trails.

Among the many others who have provided me with useful material are L.G.D. Ogden, Life Vice President of the County AAA; the late R.M. Wight of Leicester University; Ann Bray, County AAA; Kenneth Bray, English Schools AA; George Cole, Leisure Services Dept., Leicester City Council; E.E. Snow and D. Deedman of Leicestershire County Cricket Club; Lt. Col. J. Wilson of the Tigers' Association; Dr M. Tozer of Uppingham School; programmes of the late Jim Wesley; and R. Gosai of Belgrave Residents' Association. Invaluable assistance has also been provided by Aubrey Stevenson, Local Studies Librarian; the staff of Leicestershire County Record Office and Leicester University Library; Mona McKay of Loughborough University Library; and Jane Legget, formerly of Newarke Houses Museum, Leicester. Many thanks must also go to Peter Leeson of the former Urban Studies Centre in Leicester, who over a decade ago encouraged the concept of a local athletics history.

I am particularly grateful to Jack Buckner and the Race Walking Record *for permission to quote from publications; to George Herringshaw, the* Leicester Mercury, *and the family of the late Alfred Adcock for photographs; and to Sebastian Coe MP for contributing the Foreword to this book. Final thanks go to the Living History Unit of Leicester City Council, in particular to Cynthia Brown for editing the text, to Mandy Freer for typing it, and to Ian Gregson for additional research items.*

T.J.S.

FOREWORD BY SEBASTIAN COE - THE WORLD 800M RECORD HOLDER

I look back with fond memories of the time I spent in Leicestershire in the late 70's and early 80's. The Loughborough campus was ideal for training. On the soft level grass it was possible to run for over four uninterrupted miles. Since then, of course, there have been understandable incursions into the campus: new buildings and the Epinal Way!

There were other well positioned natural running areas close by. The Outwoods provided a number of popular routes through to Beacon Hill. Bradgate Park served not only as a good source of hill repetition running but also as a picturesque change from the monotony of heavy mileage during the winter months.

I look forward with great interest to reading Jim Sharlott's history of athletics in Leicester. His knowledge and understanding of the sport within the county are second to none.

Sebastian Coe

Best Wishes
S.N.C.

SELECT CHRONOLOGY

1787 Foot racing said to be "much in fashion" in Leicester (*Leicester Journal*).

1825 Wharf Street Cricket Ground opened. Also hosted general sports, concerts and other entertainments. Closed 1860.

1859 First Uppingham School sports.

1863 Oldest known athletics trophy in Leicester awarded.

1865 National Olympian Society founded in Liverpool.

1866 Olympic Festival, Leicester (May), Olympic Festival, Crystal Palace, London (Aug)

1867 First Stoneygate School sports, continuing to the present day.

1872 First known instance of a starting gun used in England, at Leicester and Leicestershire Athletic Sports, Belgrave.

1878 Opening of Aylestone Cricket Ground, with cinder track around perimeter for cycling and running.

1880 Formation of national AAA and Midland Counties AAA. Belgrave Road Grounds opened by Col. Fred Burnaby. First Leicester Infirmary Sports.

1901 National cross country championships held at Oadby Racecourse.

1903 Leicester Harriers founded. George Brewin (L'boro) first local winner of AAA title (200 yds)

1907 Road Walking Association founded.

1912 Formation of International Amateur Athletics Federation.

1919 Formation of Leicestershire AAA at Granby Halls, first county association in country under new scheme. Formation of Inter-University Athletics Board.

1920 A.R. Mills, DCM, first Leicester athlete (Leicester Harriers) in International Cross Country Championship, Belfast.

1922 Women's AAA founded.

1927 Formation of Leicestershire Schools AA, and first championships. Leicester Mercury road walk. Inaugural winner T. Lloyd Johnson. Leicester Walking Club founded.

1928 Livingston road relay inaugurated. First six feet high jump in city at Wolsey Sports. First recorded use of loud speakers at sports in Leicester.

1929 First Runners V Walkers race, held at Blackbird Road dog stadium.

1931 Alfred Adcock, first local English Schools champion. Leicester sisters Ruth Christmas and Mrs. E. Raven run for England in first cross-country international. First Colleges of Art and Technology sports, Blackbird Road playing fields.

1932 Ruth Christmas runs fastest GB 800m in Dusseldorf.

1934 British Amateur Athletics Board established to select national teams. Inter Counties track and field championships leave London for Loughborough. Mrs. W Fisher, first lady starter in Leicestershire.

1937 Loughborough College stadium and cinder track opened.

1940 British United (Business House) youths win wartime Midland cross country championship. 2 T. Sharlott, 3 T. Baggott, 10 P.Loakes.

1946 Formation of North Midlands cross country league, founder secretary, George White. Leicester Walking Club's first Centurion, Chris Clegg. County secretary Fred Cox retires after 28 years. Succeeded by L. G. D. Ogden.

1948 En-tout-cas build Wembley Olympic track in record time. Tebbs Lloyd Johnson, age 48, wins bronze medal in 50k walk in London Olympics. Reorganisation of County AAA.

1950 Leicester University College Ground, Manor Road, Oadby, opened. Leicester Schools Athletic Association formed.

1951 Leicester University College host County AAA Championships at Manor Road.

1952 Saffron Lane grass track, cycling and athletics.

1958 First Leicester Skegness 100-mile walk, won by Wilf Smith (LWC).

1960 Leicestershire Secondary Schools' first cross country league race at Lutterworth (founder secretary, Reginald Burton).

1964 Tokyo Olympics. John Cooper wins silver medals in 400m hurdles and relay.

1967 Opening of Saffron Lane Sports Centre by the Duchess of Gloucester. County championships move from Manor Road to Stadium.

1968 Five Star schools award scheme (County agent, David Couling). County Schoolgirls make debut in All-England cross country inaugural at Rochdale. AAA 10-mile championship at Saffron Lane, won by Ron Hill.

1969 County clubs merge to form one big club, Leicester Coritanians.

1970 GB V West Germany, under 20 international at Saffron Lane. Paris air disaster - John Cooper and Jack Burtonwood (father of Jenny Burtonwood, later county champion and coach) killed. Women's Inter Counties meeting for Jackson Trophy, Saffron Lane. John Boggis of Evington takes second place in the 3000m in the European Junior Championships in Paris.

1971 Richard Callan (LC) age 15, world age best for 1500m (3-56.5).

1972 Chris Monk, sprinter, career peak: AAA 200m title in 21.1;European Cup 200m final in 21.0 (headwind); silver medal, World Student Games in 20.7; won international in Athens in 20.8. John Offord sets county 3,000m steeplechase record (heat) in AAA championship in 8-43.8 at Crystal Palace.

1975 Brian Adams wins first of five consecutive AAA 10,000m walking championships.

1977 Inaugural Leicestershire Primary Schools cross country league at Kirby Muxloe (Rob Osborn, founder secretary).

1979 First Leicester Charities marathon, Victoria Park.

1980 First of three consecutive Dairygate meetings, Saffron Lane.

1981 Leicestershire win Inter-Counties walking title at Exeter - P. Vesty, B. Adams, A. King, A. Trigg.

1982 Diana Davies (LC) UK high jump record, Oslo of 1.95m, still standing March 1994. UK indoor record, 1.94m.

1983 Leicester Coritanians junior men win their first national cross country title at Luton -

P. Makepeace, C. Mochrie, J. Parker, T. Stone. Leicester Coritanian girls under 13 win national cross country championship on Warwick racecourse.

1984 Formation of County summer road racing league, founder secretary Ted Toft.

1985 John Vincent (LWC), wins first of his five All-England Schools race walking titles. County winter road racing league established.

1987 Leicestershire Intermediate ladies win Inter-Counties Cross Country Championship at Kettering. Individual winner, Maxine Newman and 3 Helen Titterington, 8 Lisa York, 13 Melanie Wilkes.

1988 Helen Titterington becomes Leicester Coritanian's first senior National cross country champion at Leeds.

1989 Craig Mochrie becomes first Leicester born man to run sub four minute mile, at Berry Hill, Mansfield, in 3-59.6. Special Olympics held in Leicester. Formation of British Athletics Federation, a single unified governing body for the sport.

1990 John Fraser (Owls) veteran 65-69, sets world record 3000m, indoors at Cosford of 11-04.1.

1991 Leicestershire win Inter Counties 20-mile road race championship, for first time at Stafford - 2 John Grindey, 10 Steve Needs, 11 Joey Masterson.

1992 Lisa York sets All Comers one mile record (NIA Birmingham) 4-33.50. World Junior Championships, Seoul, Korea. Local competitors Matthew Hibberd (1500m), Helen Frost (400m), Carl Southam (400m).

1993 Leicestershire Interset Sports, Saffron Lane, 20th anniversary (Ann Bray). Leicester Mercury road walk, 60th year. David Payne of Leicester (Tipton) second in National cross country senior championship.

1994 Oadby and Wigston Legionnaires Young Athletes runners up in National cross country and relay championships. Fifth British United 92 miles round Leicester relay (Jim Smith).

INTRODUCTION

This is the first published outline of local track and field. It does not claim to be a complete history, but rather a series of milestones charting the course of modern athletics in and around Leicester from its 19th century origins to its most recent years.

Leicester was at the forefront of Midlands developments even before the formation of the Amateur Athletic Association (AAA) in 1880. The Leicester Athletic Society, founded in 1866, organised activities from its High Street gymnasium, to the west of the former Co-operative Society store. From here, it initiated running, jumping, throwing and walking events on a scale comparable with other parts of the country, and in May 1866 held its own "Olympiad" in the grounds of the County Lunatic Asylum.

Early athletics clubs were composed entirely of "gentlemen amateurs", distinguished by the term from the professional sprinting and race walking which were a focus of lower class betting, gambling and occasional riotous behaviour. In due course, athletic ability came to outweigh differences of social status, and by the end of the 19th century, the sport had become much less exclusive. Indeed, working class athletics were often sponsored by the Victorian middle classes themselves, anxious not only to safeguard British industrial and military efficiency and to foster a national "team spirit", but also to divert the masses from drink and other "demoralising" leisure pursuits.

The amateur v professional divide remained intact for very much longer, though as the *Leicester Athlete* noted in 1884, even the AAA itself found it virtually impossible to "draw a hard and fast line" between the two. Here we can follow the debate from a local perspective - and here too we find Leicestershire well ahead of the national field, with the formation in 1919 of the first county AAA in the country.

The development is also traced of local clubs and schools athletics, both of which have provided model examples of harmonious sporting relations. Many clubs began as harrier clubs, with track and field activities added in due course to their original cross country activities. Cross country continues to be a thriving part of local athletics, while road running has gained a new impetus since the first London Marathon in 1981. The race walking scene has been dominated since its formation in 1927 by the Leicester Walking Club, now the oldest of the local clubs since others merged in 1969 to form the Leicester Coritanians. Business houses, educational establishments, public authorities and other enthusiasts have also produced their own clubs, and their contribution is not overlooked.

Enthusiastic as they might be, athletes were often hampered by a lack of adequate facilities. The book traces the slow and often frustrating journey from the Wharf Street Cricket Ground in the 1820s to the Saffron Lane Sports Centre in the late 1960s, by way of a series of temporary expedients, and the facilities generously provided by the University of Leicester at its own ground at Manor Road, Oadby. Handicapped by the search for a suitable site and post-World War II spending restrictions, the City Council's own plans for a purpose-built stadium proceeded so slowly that at one point the Chairman of the Parks Committee publicly doubted "if I'll be alive when it is done".

The opening of the Saffron Lane Sports Centre in May 1967 marked not only the end of forty years of public campaigning for an athletics track, but a new era which brought national championships and top class athletes from other parts of Britain and beyond to Leicester. Some of the most memorable Saffron Lane meetings and performances are recalled here, among them the never-to-be forgotten occasion in 1989 when Leicester played host to the Special Olympics.

The book concludes with a survey of local Olympians, ranging from the most recent to the 1920 marathon runner Bobby Mills. Here, among an impressive array of athletes past and present, we find T. Lloyd Johnson, nine times winner of the Mercury Walk and the oldest athlete ever to win an individual Olympic medal; John Cooper, double silver medallist in Tokyo in 1964, who died tragically in the Paris air disaster ten years later; Diana Davies, holder of the UK high jump record since 1982 - and many others besides. Here, as in the book as a whole, the main focus is on Leicester, but not to the exclusion of county connections. After all, what roll of local Olympians would be complete without Charnwood AC's Jack Buckner, or ex-Loughborough University student and double gold medallist Sebastian Coe, who recalls his time in the county in the Foreword to this book.

Many other eminent athletes appear in its pages, but purely for want of space, others have inevitably received less attention than they might deserve. Their achievements are however acknowledged in the Appendices, which telescope much of the raw detail of outstanding performances, and provide a valuable statistical summary for future reference.

Jim Sharlott, the author of this book, was born in Stratford-upon-Avon, and moved to Leicester in 1937. Except for wartime service in the Royal Marines, he has lived in Belgrave ever since. An accomplished athlete and one-time boxer, he won his first prize - a case of silver spoons - in a children's race at a National Farmers Union sports when he was ten.

At Topsham in 1945 he won the South West one mile, and took first place in the half mile in the revived County Championships at Blackbird Road, Leicester, in the following year. His work as Press Secretary for Leicester Colleges of Art and Technology AC led to him being invited to report on athletics for the *Leicester Mercury*, and he has now written for the paper for around 45 years. In addition, he has regularly announced at Saffron Lane Sports Centre, and at road races in the county. Research into athletics has long been a passion, and there is space in this book for only a fraction of the material he has collected over the years. Much of it has been gathered from local newspapers from 1850 onwards, and from memorabilia and statistical records, which have been a valuable source of background information. So far as Leicestershire and Rutland AAA matters are concerned, there are no official records until 1937. A few handwritten pages cover the years to 1946, when post-war reorganisation ushered in an era of new administration, headed by L.G.D. Ogden, a leading Midlands quarter-miler.

However, the many people listed elsewhere in the acknowledgements have provided invaluable information about this and other aspects of the local scene. Photographs relating to the earlier athletics history of Leicester have unfortunately proved few and far between, but the more recent illustrations provided by sports photographer and former athlete George Herringshaw more than compensate for this deficiency.

As Sebastian Coe writes in his foreword, Jim Sharlott's knowledge and understanding of local athletics are second to none, and the Living History Unit is pleased to have this opportunity of making them available to a wider audience.

Cynthia Brown
February 1994

1 EARLY DAYS

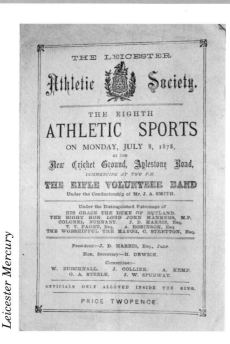

Leicester Mercury

The formation of organised clubs in the 1860s really marks the beginning of athletics in its modern form. The sport was already growing in popularity in the universities and public schools, and among army officers, and many of the founders of the early clubs were "gentlemen" from such backgrounds. Initially at least, these clubs were very exclusive, and the rules of the Amateur Athletic Club, founded in London in 1866, specifically barred "any mechanic, artisan or labourer" from membership. Social status apart, those who followed such occupations were seen as having an unfair physical advantage over the "gentlemen", but the latter were also anxious to distance athletics from professional sprint racing and pedestrianism.

FOOTRACING AND PEDESTRIANISM

As the Leicester Journal noted on 25 May 1787, both footracing and cricket were "very much in fashion" in the late 18th century.

Cricket in particular was so fiercely contested that when "Nick's roughs as some of the parishioners of St. Nicholas were called won laurels at Hinckley by defeating the players of Coventry...the Coventry players were so mortified by their defeat they incited a party of colliers to mob the Leicester players, but when the latter approached the homes they were met at the entrance to the town by an incredible concourse of inhabitants on horse and foot, and at night some of the streets of Leicester were illuminated in honour of their victory. The Leicester players received in fact such a complete ovation on the occasion they might have been winners of the OLYMPIAN GAMES". This is the earliest known local reference to footracing, but does this mention of the Olympian Games refer to the ancient Games of Greece, or much more likely, to the Robert Dover Games in the Cotswolds? The "Cotswold Olimpick Games" got under way in 1612 and were last held in 1852, more than 40 years before the present Olympiad was revived.

Both sprinting and pedestrianism had previously enjoyed aristocratic patronage, but by the mid 19th century they were regarded as lower class pursuits, associated with betting and the fixing or "roping" of races. Walter Thom's book *Pedestrianism* (1813) gives the most detailed account of the wagering, challenging and betting which accompanied the sport - and the great stamina required by competitors. Thom quotes the feat of Captain Barclay, recorded in his journal *One Thousand Miles in One Thousand Hours*. In each hour Barclay had to walk one mile. It took him 296 hours, or 12 days eight hours, to complete the thousand miles, at an average rate of 81 miles and 142 yards in 24 hours.

Though not on the same scale, in June 1853 the *Leicester Chronicle* reported a local example. "Mountjoy accomplished his task of walking from Loughborough to Derby and back, twice a day, for six consecutive days, shortly before twelve o'clock last Saturday night. He was escorted into the town by a band of music, and there were hundreds of persons in the street to witness his arrival. The distance he thus walked was 408 miles, which in the oppressive heat of last week made no easy task".

That represents an average of 68 miles a day, and is typical of other references to local pedestrianism during that period. One can imagine Mountjoy's fight against fatigue, perhaps fortified by the dope of the day, strychnine in lozenge form, or a brandy-soaked sugar lump, a high octane booster.

FOOTRACING FOR MONEY ON LEICESTER RACECOURSE

Victoria Park was in 1864 the Leicester Racecourse, and long after the move to an enclosed development in Oadby in 1883, was known locally by its original name. Cricket of a high standard was being played on the London Road pitches, for the Wharf Street Cricket Ground which had hosted Leicestershire since 1825 was shut in 1860.

Confirmation that running for money was a common occurrence in the town is contained in advertisements in the *Leicester Chronicle* and *Leicester Journal* in May 1864 for a display of forestry by the Leicester Ancient Order of Foresters, a Friendly Society in Town Hall Lane. This was staged on the racecourse on July 11 1864, and the entertainment included footracing "for a silver cup and money", as well as bands, a "wizard and magician" and Coxwell's New Mammoth Balloon. The day was an enormous success with 50,000 people attending, many conveyed by special trains, but Mr Coxwell's balloon was unfortunately destroyed by fire before it could ascend. The Foresters celebrated their 150th anniversary in 1984, and their present building is in St Nicholas Place, west of High Street.

LEICESTER "OLYMPIAD" IN 1866

However, a grand Olympic Festival on Thursday May 24 1866 in the spacious grounds of the Leicestershire and Rutland Lunatic Asylum is the major starting point for athletics in Leicester. It was organised by the newly-formed Leicester Athletic Society, and consisted of 15 events, with supporting activities such as gymnastics, fencing and a demonstration of skills with Indian Clubs.

The Asylum grounds, on a site of 37 acres, were set out in walks, pleasure gardens, allotments and parkland for the exercise of patients. The Asylum itself was designed by local architect William Parsons, and survives today as the Fielding Johnson Building of the University of Leicester. This takes it name from the benefactor Thomas Fielding Johnson, who in 1919, having concluded a secret purchase of grounds and buildings for £40,000, handed them over for the establishment of a University College. There is now a school cricket field on the site, running parallel to Welford Road, which was originally farmland. That is most probably the place where Leicester's first Olympiad was held.

The size and scale of the meeting embracing track and field events, were advanced, and pre-suppose that athletics activities were already well-established. In the Midlands we have long paid homage to Dr Penny Brookes, an influential advocate for the revival of the ancient Olympic Games. At Much Wenlock, Shropshire, in 1850, he staged his own Games. The athletics contests were modest, restricted to three foot races and a high and long jump. A decade later other events were added. One wonders though, in the light of circumstantial evidence, whether the Leicester meeting had received inspiration from Dr Penny Brookes.

A National Olympian Society was formed in Liverpool in 1862. According to a report of the event, "a National Society is about to be formed for the encouragement of Athletic Exercises in England. One thousand pounds a year is to be subscribed for distribution in prizes. The meetings are to be held annually at or near one of the Principal Cities or Towns in Great Britain. The Society is not to confine its attention to athletics exercises. It is to pay homage to Poetry, Sculpture, Painting etc. by awarding its medals".

The National Olympian Association scheduled its first meeting for August 1866, at Crystal Palace. It was to be the role model for others to emulate. But Leicester jumped the gun and organised an occasion of high class entertainment.

The May 24 meeting in Leicester enjoyed quality patronage, including the Mayor, T.W. Hodges, Esq., Samuel Stone, 36 years Town Clerk of Leicester, hosiery manufacturer Joseph Whetstone, and the Rev. J.O. Picton, of Gallowtree Gate Chapel, now the site of Boots the Chemists. Others included John Buck, Medical Superintendent of the Asylum who gave permission for the use of its grounds, and Thomas Tertius Paget, banker and Borough Treasurer.

Gentlemen who wished to enter but who were not members of the Leicester Athletic Society "may learn all particulars at the Gymnasium, 79 High Street, Leicester, on Tuesday and Thursday." Admission to the ground was by ticket only, obtainable from J. and J. Vice, Bible and Crown, Market Place; Mr J.A. Smith, Music Warehouse, King Street, and from members of the Society. Prices were one shilling to the ground and two shillings to the stand. No money was to be taken at the gate, which would ensure the exclusion of the casual man in the street.

The meeting was clearly for gentlemen of particular strata in Leicester society and names of competitors and spectators include well known families of the period, such as Worthington, Underwood, Harris and Stafford. The location of the venue, so near to New Walk, Stoneygate and Knighton, burgeoning fashionable residential areas, was an assurance that the desired people would find it convenient to attend. Nationally there were other pointers to a class interest in that period, not least in the amateur/professional divide, discussed more fully elsewhere.

Starter at the meeting was Mr Wells. The Mr distinction is important where Esquire is the norm and represents the epitome of Gentlemen and Players. Mr Wells was in trade as a cricket, running, lawn tennis and cycling footwear specialist, on Belgrave Road, in the vicinity of the bygone Great Northern Station, now occupied by Sainsbury's.

J.D. Thompson, Secretary of the Leicester Athletic Society, won the 100 yards in 11 seconds flat, from R.H. Worthington and J.A. Underwood. He also took part in the throwing of the hammer, an event graphically reported in the *Leicester Chronicle and Mercury United*. "This feat was one that excited considerable interest......... The competitor who took the first innings, either through not having sufficiently observed his position or taken a false step in turning, sent the hammer with tremendous force to the right of the ring instead of to the front, caused it to fall foul of a lady's dress as she having noted the direction of the hammer, was escaping with others out of danger. Fortunately the rather formidable weapon was observed in time, or fearful consequences might have been the result of this mishap.

EGYPTIAN FOOT POWDER for athletes 'speedily gives the greatest ease, and cures Tender Feet, gradually checking excessive perspiration from the feet without injury to the system', according to an advertisement in the *Leicester Athlete and Midland Counties Bicycle News* in March 1884. A small size packet sold for 6d. (2.5 pence).

"A wider berth was given to the remaining competitors who threw the hammer astonishingly long distances, but the nervous excitement which had been caused, was scarcely allayed till this amusement was succeeded by something less dangerous. The contest resulted in favour of Simpson by long odds, the distance which he threw the hammer being 31 yards 2 ½ feet."

The hammer in question would weigh 16 lbs and have a wooden handle four feet long. It could have been thrown from between two lines or a circle. Later rule changes included the adoption of the piano wire to replace the handle. Nevertheless it was a lethal implement and was made a safer event in 1927 with the introduction of a hammer cage in Britain. The ladies were fortunate in escaping in their long skirts and bustles, for there are on record several reports of fatal accidents from free flying hammers.

The size of the running track or lap, based on the number of circuits quoted for the two miles walk would be 293.3 yards or six laps to the mile. There is no indication of which direction athletes would run - left or right hand in or where the stands were located. Early prints show stands in the centre of arenas, but there were no photographs in newspapers in Leicester in 1866. There is no mention either of a landing area for long or high jumpers or of a water jump in the steeplechase.

Along with the winning times, it is worth noting the wide range of events, which included a 'Pole Leap':

100 yards: J.D. Thompson, 11 secs.

High jump: S. Sheen and E. Gittins, a tie; 4ft. 11ins.

Three quarter-mile steeplechase: E. Gittins, no time given.

High jump, under 18: S. Frost, 4ft 1in.

Quarter mile steeplechase, under 18: S. Forest 56 seconds.

200 yards hurdles race open: E. Gittins, $27^{1/2}$ secs.

Long jump, open: W. Bunney, distance not given.

Two miles walking race: J.G. Crofts, 18mins 3secs.

Putting the Stone: J.D. Thompson, 29ft. 3ins.

Quarter-mile flat race, under 18: T. Viccars, 54secs.

Pole Leap: A.Y. Nutt, 7ft 8ins.

Cricket ball: A.Y. Nutt, $86^{1/4}$ yards.

Hammer: J. Simpson, 31 yards $2^{1/2}$ feet.

One mile flat: J.D. Thompson, 5 minutes.

Consolation stakes ($^{1/4}$ mile race with hurdle jumps): C. Kirby.

OLDEST KNOWN ATHLETICS TROPHY IN LEICESTER

Some athletics clubs were set up as a means of keeping fit for other sports such as rugby football, and the Leicester Athletic Society had its own rugby team in the early 1870s. According to a report of a match against St. Margaret's, "The second fifteen of the Leicester Athletic Society should have played the Leicester Amateurs, but as a sufficient number did not turn up, eight of the Amateurs joined the St. Margaret's, making a total of 23 men against 17 of the Leicester Athletic Society".

Other athletic societies - like that in Liverpool - had close ties with the Rifle Corps, a national network of volunteers consisting largely of country gentry and local businessmen. The oldest known athletics trophy in Leicester, won by Henry Stocks Platts in 1863, was itself awarded by the Rifle Volunteers.

The trophy belongs to Henry Stocks Platts' granddaughter, and was once used as a flower pot. The inscription on the trophy, 300 yards, was not immediately accepted as referring to a running race. The distance of 300 yards will be familiar to many who have served in HM Forces and relates to a rifle range distance. In *The Times* of November 20 1860, there is a letter from J. Earle Brown of the Newarke, Leicester, on the subject of firing a rifle, in which he writes: "There can be no doubt that it is essential to increase the number of first class marksmen among our Volunteers at longer distances than 200, 300 or even 500 yards."

Stocks Platts lived in Loughborough, and the inscription on the trophy, 6th L.R.V. is the abbreviation for a Loughborough based company of the Leicestershire Rifle Volunteers. Captain F.A.M. Webster, a prolific writer on athletics who was on the pre-war staff at Loughborough College, had with his Army background taken a keen interest in Volunteers. In his book, *The Growth of Modern Athletics* (1929), he wrote about one of the great champions of the past: "Mr Walter Rye, London Athletic Club, died in 1929 at the age of 85 years. He was the oldest living champion. He ran his first race in 1861 when seventeen and a half years old in a 300 yards contest, Fulham, in connection with a Volunteer Fete, but fell when lying third."

Here is a specific reference to the Volunteers running 300 yards races, at exactly the same period when Henry Stocks Platts won his trophy. There is no knowledge of Platts being a member of the Volunteers, but with known Volunteers athletics activities in Loughborough, the weight of evidence is in favour of it being for running rather than firing a rifle.

THE INFIRMARY SPORTS

In the later 19th century, athletics meetings were often an occasion for fund-raising for local charities. Foremost among them were the annual sports in aid of the Leicester Infirmary, which was supported solely by voluntary subscriptions and donations until 1948.

The first Infirmary Sports were held in September 1880 at the instigation of Mr J.P. Greaves of the Leicester Bicycle Club and Mr Major of the *Mercury*. Subsequent events were organised by the Infirmary Sports Committee, which was affiliated to both the Midland Counties AAA and the National Cyclists Union. One of the Infirmary treasurers, the well-known local businessman Alfred Corah, was himself a Vice-President of the Leicestershire Athletics and Cycling Club, and Tom Crumbie, Secretary of Leicester Football Club for thirty three years from 1895, regularly acted as gate steward for the sports. F.C. Toone was official handicapper for many years, and gave a shield for a Boys 150 yards championship to be contested as part of the proceedings.

In the later 19th century the Infirmary Sports were held at the Aylestone Ground. In 1892 admission cost 6d. (2.5 pence), within the means of many working class families at that time, or 5s. (25 pence) for the special reserved enclosure. The Highfields Brass

Band provided music for the sports themselves and for dancing in the evening, and £500 was contributed to Infirmary funds that year, bringing the total to date to £3000. In 1884 competitors paid an entry fee of 2s. 6d. (12.5 pence) per event, effectively excluding all but "gentlemen" from competing.

Events in that year included 120 and 250 yards handicaps, one and three mile bicycle handicaps, and a one mile tricycle race. According to the *Leicester Athlete and Midland Counties Bicycle News*, the sports were a great success. It was "next to impossible for the keepers of the turnstiles to cope with the thousands of spectators anxious to gain admission.... Everything passed off without a hitch, except the last race, when the people crowded round the water jump in such numbers as to prevent the steeplechase being run until a great number of persons had left the ground".

Many famous athletes competed at the Infirmary Sports and other Leicester meetings. One was Lord Burghley. Another was Bill Sturgess (London Polytechnic), winner of eight AAA walking titles. Yet another, Joe Binks of London (Unity AC), was British mile record holder for many years, and later the noted athletics correspondent of the *News of the World*.

The Institute for the Blind also benefited from an annual athletics meeting. At the eighth such gathering in 1892, the *Leicester Daily Post* reported, "the handicapping was exceptionally good, and much of the racing, as a natural consequence, well worth seeing. The judging likewise left little to be desired, which isn't always the case with amateurs who get very little practice at the game".

THE TIGERS SPORTS

Both Leicester Football Club and Leicester Fosse F.C. (now Leicester City) staged athletics meetings to raise funds for their own organisations, though in the later 19th century they faced increasing competition from Bank Holiday rail excursions to the East Coast. The May 1899 Sports also suffered from "atmospheric conditions strongly resembling November". However, Minute Books from the Leicester F.C. Sports Committee in 1897 provide a useful guide to the organisation of athletic sports at the turn of the century.

Amongst other things, they show how well the Tigers and Leicester Fosse co-operated with each other - although there was a year when both wanted the same ground on the same date! Sharing the costs of ropes, tents and decorations are examples of how they kept expenses down: "The tender of Mr Mitchell re Decorations and Illuminations was accepted providing the cost does not exceed £7. It was thought advisable to arrange with

Wheelbarrow Race Society: the "big push" at the Society for the Blind Sports at the Belgrave Road ground in 1893. (Leicester Mercury)

the Fosse Sports Committee to share part of this expense".

The Leicestershire County Cricket Club ground at Grace Road was hired for an agreed 10% of the gate. The Highfields Band provided music during the meeting, and it was stipulated that they march to the venue along a designated route, drumming up support on the way. Double bills were posted on the Leicester trams on Friday, Saturday and Whit Monday, and advertisements placed in the sporting press. Entry forms were also distributed at the Nottingham Forest F.C. Sports, a meeting still in existence at the beginning of World War II.

Prizes were displayed at Snaith's, designers and decorators, in Granby Street, and a tender for the privilege of selling "hokey", a local name for ice cream, was accepted from Mr Massarella. Programmes were printed by Tom Crumbie, and F.C. Toone once again acted as handicapper. The meeting was conducted strictly to Midland Counties AAA rules, and events included 120 and 220 yards flat handicaps, a 1000 yards steeplechase, bicycle handicaps, "comical races", and a tug-of-war "open to Leicestershire teams". As well as Whitsun events, sports were often held in September before the start of the rugby season.

CYCLE RACING AND ATHLETICS

As the title of the Leicester Athlete and Midland Counties Bicycle News *suggests, cycling was at least as popular as athletics in the later 19th century, and by the 1890s cycle racing had become a major spectator sport. Bicycle races and athletics were often featured in the same meetings and combined in the same club.*

At the Infirmary Sports in 1891, Bert Harris, Champion Amateur Track Cyclist of England, "rode magnificently. He was the hero of the afternoon, the youthful rider setting a great pace on his machine, and splendidly maintaining his reputation as one of the very fastest riders in England today". In due course, Harris - who lived in Belgrave - abandoned his amateur status and became Champion Professional of England.

The Leicestershire Athletic and Cycling Club formed in 1895, held Sports and Schoolboys championships on the Aylestone Grounds. Held in high esteem, its patrons included Lord Lonsdale of Barleythorpe Hall in Rutland, Lord Cecil Manners, MP, and Lord Edward Manners of Belvoir, the Earl of Denbigh, and Sir Israel Hart, JP. Club President was Sir John Rolleston MP, and Alfred Corah, Frank Toone and G.W. Hillyard, enhanced its status. Hillyard, of Thorpe Satchville, Leics., won the men's doubles tennis championship at the 1908 London Olympics at the age of 44, partnered by R.F. Doherty.

Cycle racing, as an advertisement in the Leicester Athlete pointed out in 1884, was not the safest of sports: "To Cyclists. Accidents will happen!! It may be your turn next, so provide against Loss through Total or Partial Disablement by insuring in the Imperial Union Accident Co." Bert Harris himself died tragically at the age of 23 after falling and hitting his head on the concrete track during a cycle race in Birmingham in 1897. His monument in Welford Road Cemetery in Leicester was placed there

"BY THE CYCLISTS OF ENGLAND, AS A TOKEN OF THE SINCERE RESPECT AND ESTEEM IN WHICH HE WAS HELD BY WHEELMEN THE WORLD OVER. HE WAS EVER A FAIR AND HONOURABLE RIDER AND SPORTSMAN AND HIS LAMENTED DEATH CUT OFF IN HIS PRIME ONE OF THE BRIGHTEST AND MOST GENIAL SPIRITS OF CYCLEDOM".

THE LEICESTER RECORD

Further glimpses of the local athletics scene can be found in the Leicester Record, a small booklet published for three consecutive years between 1887-89 by Pickard, Valentine & Co. of Rutland Street, Leicester. Only one known copy survives, privately owned.

Its pages are packed with detailed results of professional and amateur athletics, cycling, swimming, roller skating and rowing. The athletics season was not divided into winter cross country and summer track and field: as late as December, there was a 100 yards match on Victoria Park. Both the Belgrave Road and Aylestone Grounds also featured events over various distances. No times are quoted for the foot races, but in cycling, results are declared to a fifth of a second.

At the Belgrave Road Grounds, runners and cyclists could practice for one penny (240 to £1 in pre-decimal coinage), or buy quarterly, half-yearly and yearly tickets for 5s 6d (27p.), 10s 6d (52p.) and one guinea (£1.05) respectively. It was also possible to buy tickets for cricket matches, and a clubhouse on the ground provided refreshments of all kinds. Trotting events were held in conjunction with some sports meetings - admission for one horse and a man for practice cost 6d (2p) and included "excellent stabling". There are advertisements for prizes and liniments, and for chronographs, early stop watches available from Botts in Gallowtree Gate at a cost of £1 to £50. Mr Wells, the starter in the first Olympiad at the Asylum in 1866, also features, advertising his wares as a specialist boot and shoe maker on Belgrave Road.

There were several athletics clubs in existence at this time, most of them known as harrier clubs, with origins in cross country running rather than track and field. A local list includes the Leicester, St. George's, Temperance, Aylestone Park, Victoria, Tally Ho and East Leicester Harriers, and the Leicester Amateur Cross Country Association.

THE "DUMMY TOWN" STARTING GUN

The first known report of a starting gun in Leicester was at Belgrave - otherwise known as "Dummy Town" - in August 1872. This date precedes by four years the instance given of its initial use in the Guiness Book of Athletics Facts and Feats *(1984).*

"1876: Starting gun first used; previously races started with a drum, or 'go', or a white handkerchief", it states under "Milestones in Athletics History". However, the *Leicester Chronicle and Leicester Mercury United* of August 31 1872 gives an earlier mention of the use of a starting gun, in a report of the Leicestershire Athletics Sports and Pony

Races in Belgrave.

"This annual gathering commenced on Monday last on a field in the parish of Belgrave near to Birstall Lane. There was not more than 2000 persons present on Monday, whereas on the first day last year, when the sports were held in a field near the Borough Lunatic Asylum, there could not have been less than 6000 spectators." This more fashionable venue, on the edge of Stoneygate, may help to account for the higher numbers.

However, conditions were far from ideal in 1872. The "thick and drizzling rain" falling at the start of the sports later turned into "perfect torrents, and caused the spectators to run helter-skelter to the canvas tents... The storm raged with great fury for the space of twenty minutes... the thunder resembling the discharge of a battery of artillery near at hand...." Some events were postponed until the following day, "under the most auspicious circumstances, the weather being fine, and the spectators still more numerous than on the preceding day".

Among the events was a two mile walking race, although according to the newspaper, "it would have been more appropriately designated a 'running match'. The only competitor in the race who paid strict regard to the rule that the walking must be 'Heel and toe' was Simmonds, who deservedly won the 'First Prize'.

As late as 1939, in a field on the Belgrave side of the River Soar, young men used to gamble illegally, at cards, spinning coins, and racing whippets. A police trap was one day sprung - the look out was missing and the lads were hauled off for questioning. After failing to get any responses from the Belgrave gang, a policeman is believed to have made the remark - "What can you expect, they come from Dummy Town."

Undoubtedly this meeting attracted professional sprinters from all over the country and also provided amateur type awards, cups, goblets etc., which would be cherished from the locality.

The reference to the starting gun comes in the report of the Handicap Quarter of a Mile on the first day of the sports:

"ON THE PISTOL BEING FIRED, THE SIX COMPETITORS BEGAN DRAWING NEARER EACH OTHER, BUT HOLLIS REMAINED SLIGHTLY IN FRONT."

This question of the starting pistol was put to Mr Douglas Poli, of the Belgrave Gun Co. Ltd., who started business in Marfitt Street, Belgrave, in 1946. He suggested that the gun would have been a muzzle loading pistol, probably bought from H. Clarke and Sons, Gunmaker, who had premises at 20 Humberstone Gate and 37b Gallowtree Gate, in Leicester. No special attention was drawn to the use of a starting pistol in the newspaper report, and it may well have been used even before 1872.

2 THE LEICESTERSHIRE AAA

 *The national Amateur Athletic Association (AAA) was founded in 1880 to bring together the various bodies administering the sport. Regional associations grew up at the same time, among them the Midland Counties AAA, which included the area of Leicester and the county. The national body was governed by representatives of the major clubs and associations, including the Amateur Athletic Club of London, Cambridge and Oxford Universities, and the Civil Service Athletic Club. Its first Rules for Competition, which became the basis for later international rules, were laid down in 1889.*

AMATEURS AND PROFESSIONALS

Unlike the Amateur Athletic Club, the AAA did not exclude all but "gentlemen" from the sport, but it did make strenuous efforts to preserve its amateur status. By its own definition, "No person shall be considered an amateur who has ever competed with, or against, a professional for any prize; who has ever taught, pursued or assisted in the pursuit of Athletic Exercises of any kind as a means of livelihood".

However, as the *Leicester Athlete and Midland Counties Bicycle News* reported in March 1884, it was not so easy "to draw a hard and fast line between amateurs and professionals", and the trophies and other prizes awarded to athletes were themselves seen as undermining their amateur status. When athletics were first introduced at the Universities, the prizes offered were so small that "little inducement was held out to the competitors, beyond that of honour attaching to the victory". Now, first class athletes were said to be able to make a living by selling their prizes, and clubs able to offer large prizes were "sure to receive a greater number of entries than where only nominal prizes were given".

The value of prizes at the Leicester Infirmary Sports in 1884 ranged from 10 guineas (£10.50) to one guinea (£1.05), and were "guaranteed to be of the full advertised value". Those at the 17th Annual Loughborough Sports in the same year - "Held under AAA Rules" - were more modest at £6 for the first place and £2 for second. The AAA prohibited prizes of over £10, except for challenge cups, and also banned professional handicaps from inclusion in amateur meetings. Both moves were unpopular with promoters and were often ignored, but the AAA also prosecuted a number of athletes for accepting appearance money, and banned the payment of travelling expenses until 1899.

In the opinion of the *Leicester Athlete*, however, being a professional athlete "is no disgrace whatever in a man, as it simply means that he is willing to come before the public in his true form.............it seems impressed upon the minds of some people that the moment a man turns professional, he loses all caste with his friends".

SIZING UP SPRINTER JIM WESLEY

The Midland Counties AAA Annual Report of 1904 also shows concern for false statements and misleading information given on boys' handicap forms. The handicap was framed according to age and height, and to prevent abuses a new rule made it compulsory to have a measuring stick on the ground at all meetings.

A programme from the same year lists ages, heights and individual colours of competitors. Local sprinter Jim Wesley, at 12 years and one month, was four feet two and a half inches tall. He was the smallest boy in his heat, and off seven yards was conceding four yards start to the limit man, P.S. Jones of Leicester.

The handicapping system in adult races is based on allowances for starts and penalties for success. In a mile handicap, the limit man - the one receiving the biggest start - could be on an allowance of 190 yards. This would be reduced by 15 yards when an athlete won, and each time he won or came second or third, he would be "pulled" accordingly. If he reached the absolute starting line, he would be the "scratch" man - or more likely, the back marker, if he was the runner in receipt of the smallest allowance.

LEICESTERSHIRE AAA - ALONE ON THE STARTING LINE

County Amateur Athletic Associations were formed after the First World War under a scheme for "reconstruction". The Leicestershire AAA, founded less than three months after the guns were silenced on November 11 1918, was the first such organisation in the country.

Leicester Harrier secretary Fred Cox, twice a Midland 440 yds. champion, invited a number of Leicester sportsmen to a meeting at the Junior Training Hall (later Granby Halls), on February 4 1919. Mr Evan Barlow, a local solicitor, chaired the meeting. Evan Barlow, who died shortly before the Second World War, was among those responsible for building the Junior Training Hall. A hockey player as well as an athlete, his family still has a silver snuff box presented to him when he won a handicap running race in a Territorial Army contest.

Most important in the recommendations was the use of general control. Malpractices abounded. Betting was prohibited at athletic meetings under AAA laws, but bookmakers and their touts were in constant attendance. Handicap running was the norm, with prize values of up to seven guineas, more than twice the average wage for some working class men. To obtain a good allowance from the handicapper, athletes deliberately did not attempt to win, until they had worked their mark up to the maximum, while bookmakers bought off favourites. So in 1919 when the city sportsmen met in Granby Halls it was in the hope they could clean up some of the undesirable features.

Mr Barlow said they were meant to do whatever lay in their power to foster amateur sport. It must be clean, wholesome sport and as free from the attendant vices as it was possible to make it. Fred Cox then read out the proposals drawn up by the reconstruction committee and they were accepted. He was appointed Hon. Secretary and held the post until his retirement in July 1947. Sir Samuel Faire, managing director of Faire Bros. in Rutland Street, was invited to become President.

Once again, however, the city and county proved to be ahead of the field. "Mr Justice Shearman (Sir Montague), being President of the AAA, was delighted to meet a number of the officials of our County AAA last week", reported Fred Cox in the *Sports Mercury* on June 21 1919, "especially as the new reconstruction idea is his own pet scheme. We in our turn were proud to announce that we were first in the field to form a County organisation, with every object in view that was proposed by the parent body. We shall work the harder after his Lordship's kind interest."

In October of that year the *Sports Mercury* reported that the Leicestershire AAA was still "the only one yet formed under the new scheme, and it should be interesting to hear what the other 38 Counties have to say about it."

FIRST LEICESTERSHIRE AAA CHAMPIONSHIPS 1919

The need to hold County Championships was one of the first questions to be addressed by the Committee. There had of course been Leicestershire championships from the misty past, but they had no AAA status. The first Leicestershire AAA sports, which were also the first County AAA Championships in the country, were held on June 9 1919.

These Athletic and Cycling Sports were held at the County Cricket Ground, Leicester, and attended by a big Whit Monday holiday crowd. The 80 yards handicap for boys under 14 was easily the most popular event. It attracted an entry of 157, divided into 20 heats.

The honour of becoming the first 100 yards champion of Leicestershire belongs to Horace Arrowsmith. He won by two yards from J. Eady (Market Harborough) and A.R. Mumford (Birchfield Harriers). In the weekly notes of *Leicester Evening Mail*, "On track and path, by Sprinter," the event is spotlighted a week later. "On this running it is a pity that Owen James had not entered the 100 yards championship of Leicestershire on the Monday. I understand that he thought he was not eligible to compete." James was then named as the winner of the 100 and 220 yards handicaps at the Leicester Fosse F.C. Sports.

James hailed from Barrow-on-Soar, and died in America in 1984, aged 86. Before he emigrated, James won many local events. He was credited with being an even timer - a 100 yards in 10 seconds man. He was gassed while serving with the Horse Artillery in France, but recovered well enough to enjoy an outstanding sprinting career.

Leicestershire championships continued up to the outbreak of World War II in September 1939. In 1946, the biggest number of championship events held on one day were staged at Blackbird Road playing fields, the home ground of the Leicester Colleges of Art and Technology AC. The ground had a distinct slope, the grass was thick, and several days heavy downpour had made conditions miserable. Except for a hiccup in 1950 when no championships were held at all, because of the difficulty in obtaining a ground, the meeting has continuously developed. In recent years, a grand two day meeting involving over a hundred titles has been staged at Saffron Lane Sports Centre, Leicester.

NOTIONS OF RESPECTABLE WOMANHOOD

The AAA took no responsibility for women's athletics, and this had no governing body of its own until the formation of the Women's Amateur Athletic Association (WAAA) in 1922. Before the First World War, athletics was very much a male sport. The "dress, exertion and freedom of movement which athletics entailed were hardly compatible with notions of respectable womanhood", and it was also said to have adverse effects on women's health and their ability to have children.

The often strenuous work done by women during World War I went some way to change these views, although the first female athletes did not compete in the Olympics until 1928, and the first British women not until 1932. Even then, women were excluded from some events for many years. The women's 800 metres featured in the Amsterdam Olympics in 1928, but did not reappear until 1960 in Rome. The women's marathon was first included in 1984, but they are still barred from competing in some events, including the triple jump and pole vault.

Ruth Christmas, perhaps the earliest example of an outstanding local female athlete, was a member of London Olympiads, the first women's athletics club in the UK. On March 19 1932, as the Sports Mercury reported, both she and her sister, Mrs E. Raven,

Diana Davies (LC), UK high jump record holder and WAAA champion 1986. (George Herringshaw)

"were members of the English Women's cross country team that today met France in the first international race between the countries in England". England won the race, held at Selsdon, near Croydon, scoring 14 points to the 22 of France. "Recently, Miss Christmas ran second in the British national championship at Coventry with her leg bandaged heavily", the paper continued, "and today she once more ran the course with bandages from the ankle upwards". Gladys Lunn of England won in 12 15 $^{3/5,}$ with Ruth Christmas fourth in 13 18, and Mrs Raven sixth in 13 42.

The previous year, France, Belgium and England had met in an international cross country meeting at Douai on March 22, 1931 when Lunn, Styles and Christmas finished first, second and fourth. Ruth Christmas was an outstanding track runner too, and F.A.M. Webster in his *Athletics of Today* (1929) notes that "Miss Christmas who was second to Fraulien Dollinger at 800m in returning 2 mins. 23$^{4/5}$ ths secs. made a faster time than any British runner before her." The match in question was at Dusseldorf, Germany V Great Britain. Ruth ran second in the women's national at Wolverhampton, beaten by 16 seconds by Miss Lillian Styles.

OFFICERS AND OFFICIALS

Many officers have served the Leicestershire AAA with distinction since its formation in 1919. Foremost among them are Fred Cox, its long-serving first Hon. Secretary, and S.H.B. Livingston, initiator of the Livingston Road Relay Race, who served as President for 30 years between 1934-64. Local manufacturers like Livingston feature prominently in the list of early County Presidents, but in more recent years the office has often been filled, on an annual basis, by athletes or officers from local clubs.

The following is a full list of County AAA Presidents:

1919	Sir Samuel Faire JP	*Managing Director, Faire Bros.*
1926	Tom Hatton	*Entrepreneur, Blackbird Road Dog Stadium*
1932	Sidney Charles Packer	*Founder member of Leicester Walking Club*
1934	Samuel H. B. Livingston	*President, Leicestershire County Cricket Club*
1964	J.A. Wagstaff	*Athlete and footballer*
1965	Len Shipman CBE	*Chairman City FC and Football Association*
1967	John Smith	*Joint MD Kirby and West Dairy*
1974	Sam Kellock	*Leicester Harriers.*
1982	Ernie Boot	*Team Manager, English Cross Country Union.*
1987	Stan Dawson	*Leicester Harriers. Half mile champion and coach*
1988	Jim Sharlott	*County half mile and South West mile champion*
1989	Eric Gamble	*Long serving Treasurer of County AAA*
1990	Ted Toft	*Road racing and real cross country innovator .*
1991	Peter Adams	*Prolific worker for L W C and all AAA affairs*
1992	June Clarke	*Leicester Coritanians coach and manager.*
1993	Gordon Ward	*Charnwood. Meeting organiser.*

In addition, Hon. Secretaries Les Ogden, Ernie Day, Cedric Angove, John Hollingworth, Alan Maddison, Ken and Ann Bray shouldered administrative burdens after World War

Brenda Gibbs (LC), 1977 WAAA champion and all time UK No 2 (1.85m), pictured at WAAA meeting at Crystal Palace in August 1977. (George Herringshaw)

II, along with long-serving Treasurer Eric Gamble.

As is noted in a report of a Committee meeting in 1939, the County AAA also provided officials for local athletics meetings. In that year they included the County and National Schools championships, the College of Art Sports, the Girls Life Brigade Sports, and the Aylestone British Legion meeting on Whit Monday.

The smooth running of track and field meetings still depends on there being available a pool of dedicated volunteers who give their services free. They may be required to officiate all day, at morning and afternoon sessions, and sometimes on grounds where there is very little protection from the elements. The list of officials is now organised on a county basis relating to areas - North, South, Midlands and so on.

The convenor for Leicestershire and Rutland is Ken Oldfield of Burbage, former long distance racing cyclist and timekeeper. Richard Float, a Chief Starter (Leicester University) and author of a booklet on starting, is Chairman of the Midlands Officials Committee. There is no space to give a full list of all the men and women who attend numerous meetings each year, but it is only right that the indispensable services they provide should be recognised.

3 CROSS COUNTRY

Many athletics clubs began life as harrier clubs, originally restricted to cross country running. Courses were marked out with paper or factory waste, with handfuls dropped at strategic points. Clubs were commonly based on Friendly Societies or public houses, where the landlord was patron, but in Leicester and elsewhere Temperance Harriers often sprang up to oppose them. By the later 19th century, in keeping with concerns about industrial and military efficiency, and attempts to persuade the working classes to spend their increasing leisure time in "rational" recreations, many churches, chapels and employers were also running their own harrier clubs.

HARRIER CLUBS IN LEICESTER

In March 1884, the Leicester Athlete and Midland Counties Bicycle News *reported that the Leicester harrier club I.O.G.T. (International Order of Good Templars) "had their usual weekly run on Saturday last. Messrs. J.H. Burbidge and T. Hubbard were despatched as hares".*

On the same day, " a club chiefly composed of the employees of Messrs. Cooper, Corah and Co., one of the largest hosiery manufacturers of that town, had a run with the St. George's (Church) men. They have, I believe, been running all through the season; but with becoming modesty have kept their doings out of print and away from the molestations of the public gaze".

The runners were not always so popular with the general public or local landowners. Races often started or finished in the main streets of the town, and "for a number of young athletes in full running attire to go at full speed through our crowded streets, the passers by wondering what it all means, is not calculated to raise a fondness for the sport in the minds of the public. If the members object to a start from a public house, surely some accommodation could be secured at a private house on the outskirts, and thus avoid the unpleasantness of being looked upon as a parcel of schoolboys seeking an opportunity for public exhibition".

RECORD SALES
Englebert Humperdink records sold by the million when he achieved singing fame. His wife is Pat Healey from Queniborough, a Midland cross country medallist with Belgrave UAC.

As the *Leicester Athlete* also reported, an eight miles cross country paper chase handicap in March 1884 had to be cancelled at the last moment "in consequence of a certain person, who name we forbear to mention, objecting to the competitors crossing the land in his occupation".

NORTH MIDLANDS CROSS COUNTRY LEAGUE FORMED IN LEICESTER

Many harrier clubs eventually adopted track events, and when field events were also taken up, they ceased to be exclusively running clubs. Cross country running continued to be an integral part of club athletics, but as George White, Captain of Leicester Colleges of Art and Technology AC, pointed out in 1946, "the ordinary programme of club social fixtures gives only limited competition, and it is the experience of competing in large fields, such as are met with in championship events which we have found to be necessary". To provide this, he proposed the formation of a cross country league in the North Midlands.

In a letter sent to eight Midland clubs in 1946, George White wrote that: "My club have felt for some time that there is a need for a competitive programme of cross country events which will provide the clubs in the North Midlands Area with the experience of team competition which is found to be necessary when running in the various championship races." Those clubs invited to take part were Leicester Harriers, Hinckley Technical College, Loughborough College, Derby and County AC, Nottingham AC, Nottingham University and Sutton in Ashfield.

In June 1946 at the Leicester Colleges of Art and Technology, then Leicester Polytechnic and now De Montfort University an inaugural meeting was convened for the purpose of forming the cross country league. It was agreed to promote North Midlands Cross Country League activities within the counties of Leicestershire, Derbyshire and Nottinghamshire. First Officers were:- President, Colin Gunn; Hon. Secretary, George White; Hon Treasurer, Ray Bateman. Subsequently a friendly social run was held at Markeaton Park, Derby, and the first league race took place at Loughborough College, on November 9 1946, for senior men only.

LCAT won the inaugural race, scorers being, Gordon Wildy, Ken Johnson, Tom Sharlott, Fred Clay and George White. However, Derby won the league championship and were so powerful that they remained champions for 21 years until their superb record was broken by LCAT Clubs from Lincolnshire and Northants came in later, and from a few dozen runners in the early years, fields grew in size to reach 466 seniors at Wollaton Park, Nottingham, in November 1987.

Youth races which had been introduced on a friendly basis were given championship status in 1951. Leicester Harriers won league honours for the four years to 1955. Boys and colts came on stream and then on November 22 1980, it was decided to admit women, by a vote of a majority of two.

Numerous top class athletes have added prestige to the League. Three greats were Geoff Saunders (Derby), Basil Heatley (Melton) and Mike Tagg (Derby). All won the international cross country championship. Track stars include Seb Coe, double Olympic gold medallist, who developed a pelvic tilt attributed to an off balance step on uneven ground. The European 5000m champion, Jack Buckner (Charnwood) won at Markeaton Park in October 1985 and Leicester's first sub four minute miler, Leicester Coritanian Craig Mochrie, was also a No. 1.

The notable ladies list features Eleanor Adams world famous ultra athlete from Sutton in Ashfield and British 100k winner, Hilary Johnson, teacher at Robert Smyth School, Market Harborough, and currently a British team manager. On the administration side, there have only been two Hon. Secs., George White from the inception until 1974, followed by genial Leicester Coritanian, Ted Toft. There are now over 40 clubs in the league. Approximately 3,000 runners take part in the four fixtures, all decided before Christmas, implementing the original idea of getting ready for the New Year Championships.

There have been some unusual moments in the league. Spartan bathing facilities prevailed at early meetings. Outside tin baths, containing hot water, cooled rapidly in low temperatures and gradually silted up. The first few in enjoyed fairly clean water, but late arrivals had the choice of going home with mud caked legs or trying to remove it in the slurry.

One race finished in the dark. Cycle lamps were used to guide in runners and there were big problems for the recorders. Foot and Mouth disease quarantined several courses, delaying the completion of the programme on a number of occasions. Finally, the league boasts the fastest pencil men in the country. President Eric Gamble and Alan Loasby of Leicester have produced the most rapid results service, all details available within minutes of the final race.

WESTERN AND BRAUNSTONE PARKS - THE SETTING FOR WORLD STARS

The county AAA have been one of the busiest organisers of major championships, a policy supported by Leicester City Council, who gave permission to use Western and Braunstone Parks. Nearby schools, New Parks, Wycliffe CC and Alderman Newton Girls, provided the accommodation which catered for thousands of athletes and supporters from all over the country.

The organising habit was established nearly a hundred years ago on the Oadby race course with the staging of the National cross country championship. The winner was world famous Alfred Shrubb in a field of 113. Shrubb, of South London Harriers, won a total of four English cross country titles and 10 AAA titles. His record for 10 miles of 50-40.6 stood for 24 years. In 1964 the numbers taking part in the senior event had risen to 853. The winner was Mel Batty, who coaches the 1993 London Marathon champion Eamonn Martin. In 1976 the National was again brought to the city, first home being Bernie Ford (Aldershot) and in 1980, the victor was Nick Rose of Bristol.

The Inter Counties cross country championships, second only in importance to the National, has three races, seniors, juniors and youths, and they have been put on locally on 15 occasions. Among the champions have been Dave Bedford, a world 10,000m record breaker, Olympic silver medallist Mike McLeod, and marathon ace Steve Jones. Steve Cram also finished high in the field on Braunstone Park. Other championships include the English Schools, their knock out cup, and Women's nationals, the first being on Western Park in 1974.

City and County officials have shouldered time-consuming burdens and, as the most experienced group, expertly presented the many showpieces. The 1964 organising Committee was at the heart of affairs for many years. They included J.A. Wagstaff (President), G.E. Boot (Chairman), C. Angove (Sec.), T.W. Crosher (Hon. Treasurer), G. White, T.J. Sharlott, the author of this book, and his brother T.G.R. Sharlott. Leicester Walking Club for many years have provided marshalls.

MIDLAND COUNTIES WOMEN'S CHAMPIONSHIP

In addition to their successes in the North Midlands League, local women have also featured prominently in the Midland Counties and National Cross Country Championships.

Pat Healey (Belgrave), Midland cross country medallist, pictured (second from right) in a club event in October 1953. Other competitors (L-R) are Jennifer Hyman, all England discus champion; Jean Phillips, county 440 yd champion 1955; Rosemary Stevenson, Belgrave champion; Elise Campbell, Midland long jump champion; Margaret Cox, county shot put champion; Jean Flint, Belgrave runner up; Marie Redhead, county 440 yd champion 1954; and Doris Nadin, sprints/middle distance. Starter is Reg Burton, county schools and club secretary. (T. J. Sharlott)

The first local girl to win a medal in the Midland Counties championships was second placed junior, Pat Healey, of Belgrave United AC, in 1957. Her mother, the late Mrs Lilian Healey, was her greatest supporter and in weather fair or foul, Mrs Healey accompanied Pat on her bicycle on long training runs on the road in the Queniborough area. Despite walking the course beforehand, Pat at one stage lost her way and eventually finished second to Kettering's Betty Loakes, who became an international half miler.

The first winner from Leicester was Pat Lowe in the senior test in 1969. A member of

35

Belgrave UAC, as a youngster Pat's career was mainly with Birchfield Harriers. Since then the following county connected runners have won individual titles. Leicester Coritanian Maxine Newman is the only athlete to have won individual titles across all four age groups.

SENIOR CHAMPIONS

1969	Pat Lowe	Birchfield Harriers
1990	Maxine Newman	L Coritanians (LC)
1991	Lisa York	LC
1992	Lisa York	LC
1993	Elaine Foster	Charnwood (CH)

JUNIORS

1983	Mary Hall	LC
1986	M Newman	LC
1989	C Allen	LC

INTERMEDIATES

1986	Helen Titterington	LC
1988	M Newman	LC
1989	Tracy Maycock	LC
1990	Karen Whetton	Ibstock/Bfd

MINORS

1974	Shirley Johnson	LC
1979	Kerry Nurse	CH
1983	M Newman	LC
1992	Lisa Worden	CH

LEICESTER CORITANIANS' REMARKABLE RECORD

Leicester Coritanians have a remarkable record in women's cross country running. Amongst other things they became the first county club to win the senior team title at Colwick Woods, Nottingham in 1981. Scorers were: 6 Katrina Butters, 7 Jenny Burtonwood, 9 Debbie Curtis, 12 Margaret Boddy (NZ).

Coritanians made their first appearance in the Women's National cross country championships on Leicester's Western Park in 1974. Their girls, 2 Shirley Johnson, 16 Karen Boyce, 35 Nina Knox, 55 Sharon Johnson, took the silver medals, but it was nine years later before they mounted the team winning rostrum. However, in addition to the stream of team successes that were to follow, two magnificent senior individual victories were recorded by Coritanians. Helen Titterington (1988) won at Leeds age 18, the youngest senior title winner for 38 years, and Olympian Lisa York, months before she went to Barcelona, won emphatically at Cheltenham.

Coritanians were overall champions (all age groups added together) in 1984, 1987, 1988, 1989. They were also the first winners of the Nelson Neal memorial trophy, presented from 1987 for the best all round club.

CORITANIAN TEAM VICTORIES

1983 Girls under 13 Warwick

15 Maxine Newman, 35 Lisa York, 19 Sarah Hockin, 45 Alison Hockin

1985 Juniors under 15 Birkenhead

7 Maxine Newman, 15 Lisa York, 19 Sarah Hockin, 21 Helen Titterington

1987 Intermediate under 17

2 M. Newman, 11 Melanie Wilkes, 14 Lisa York, 20 H Titterington

1988 Under 20 inaugural event Copthall Stadium

4 M. Newman, 5 Tracy Maycock, 8 M. Wilkes, 10 Karen Whetton

1988 Intermediates Leeds

6 M. Newman, 5 T. Maycock, 24 M. Wilkes, 53 Marie Lawrence

1989 Intermediates Birmingham
3 Ruth Ellway, 18 T. Maycock, 23 K. Whetton, 63 Rachel Lovett

REG DRAPER - "THE FOSTER OF HIS DAY"

This was the headline in the Hinckley Times *of June 5 1981 in tribute to Reginald Victor Draper, whose peak career spanned the 1930s and 40s. Though also an accomplished track athlete, Reg Draper was a notable cross country runner, and "his name was as respected and well known in the world of athletics as Brendan Foster or other top athletes of today.*

"He had natural modesty and reserve, for he always shunned the limelight, letting his achievements speak for themselves. Reg shunned offers to join more prestigious clubs being content to run for Hinckley Technical College AC. This meant, among other things, instead of having well appointed dressing rooms with showers attached, he chose to change in the stokehole of the old main building of the Technical College."

Being an amateur in those days meant there was no such thing as expenses. As well as paying their own entry fee athletes had to provide their own means of transport, which often meant that for distances of up to 30 or 40 miles a cycle was often used.

Reg won many county track and cross country championships. Spectator comment was invariably about who was going to be second to Draper. In 1935, he won his first big cross country race, the Inter Counties at Luton. In 1936, Olympic year, tendon problems affected him but he was still the official reserve for the three miles. In 1937, Reg came

Reg Draper about to win another County AAA mile at Hinckley 1937. (L-R) Stan Dawson, Ray Bateman, Reg Draper, name unknown, Jim Plant, George Hart, name unknown (possibly Birch), and Stan Eggs. (George Herringshaw)

second in the National at Stratford on Avon and earned his first international vest. In what was perhaps his most notable performance, in 1938 he won the AAA 10 mile championship by 40 yards, and representing the AAA in the three mile against Oxford and Cambridge, he was first home.

Reg was preparing for marathon in 1940 but was called up for the Army. In the famous News of the World road relays over a three miles plus course in 1943, he set a course record of 14-05 at Mitcham. In 1944 and 45, while serving in BAOR (British Army of the Rhine), Reg won the 5000 metres and numerous other command championships. Other world cross country championships saw Reg performing exceptionally well, and in Army boots, Reg won a Regional Command walking title.

Footnote: *The supreme cross country honour is to be chosen to compete in the GB team in the World IAAF championship. Previous to only only one team representing the Isles, the Home Countries entered separate teams for the International Championship.*

The following local athletes have competed in the championships from the 1920s onwards: A.R. Mills, R. V. Draper, Pat Lowe, R. Grove, P. Makepeace, C. Mochrie, N. McCaffrey, Sonia McGeorge, Helen Titterington, Lisa York, Maxine Newman, Karen Whetton, and Scott West.

4 RACE WALKING

In June 1927 the Leicester Mercury sponsored a 20 miles road walk organised by the Leicestershire AAA. Huge crowds turned out to watch, hundreds of cyclists followed the walkers, and race-walking fever became an epidemic. The Mayor, Alderman T. Walker, acted as starter, and the event was won by local walker and future Olympic competitor, T. Lloyd Johnson, in 3-1-07. Almost by popular demand, the Leicester Walking Club (LWC) was formed at Groby barely a month later. Lloyd Johnson became its first secretary.

LEICESTER WALKING CLUB

Walk competitors, officials, local sportsmen and patrons assembled in the Junior Training Hall (Granby Halls) and voted to form a club. A Leicestershire AAA novice road walk had been planned for the following Tuesday, so it was decided that they would all meet again then and invite other interested people to attend.

A seven miles race had been advertised. It was to start at the Empire Hotel, Fosse Road North, Leicester, at 7 o'clock. Each competitor was allowed an attendant and the route was from Fosse Road North to Blackbird Road, Anstey Gorse, Anstey, Newtown Linford, finishing in Groby, at the Stamford Arms in the middle of the village. Tom Hatton, President of the Leicestershire AAA was appointed referee. The race was won by 18 year old A.V. Beckett of the Horseshoe Club from Robert Hall Memorial Church in 1-00-50. He took the lead in the last mile to beat G.S. Johnson, Lloyd's younger brother, who finished in 1-02-10. Third was H.A. Medcraft 1-02-45.

At a gathering in the skittle alley in the Stamford Arms after the race, the decision to form a club was unanimous. Billy Golland was elected President and T. Lloyd Johnson, Secretary. The audience included J.T. Read, the sole surviving founder member in 1993. Mr Hatton considered those present were sufficient to form the basis of what should be one of the best walking clubs in the country. With Lloyd Johnson the National Champion to guide and direct them, they could hardly go wrong.

Subsequently, the Walking Club excelled at national level, winning many individual and team titles in addition to enjoying a top class reputation

T. Lloyd Johnson (LWC), Leicester walking legend. The oldest athlete to win an Olympic individual medal, in the 50k walk at the London Olympics in 1948, at the age of 48. (Leicester Mercury)

as organisers. Secretaries Albert Johnson and Bill Bell were particularly recognised as administrators and Peter Markham, who has travelled the world for IAAF, wrote an informative manual in his role as National Coach.

There are two peaks in team fortunes most worthy of attention. In 1981 and 1983 Leicester held all five national championships trophies over 10 miles, 20km, 35km, 50km and 100km. The counting men in 1983 were: Brian Adams, Chris Bent, Chris Berwick, Alan King, Peter Markham, Chris Smith, John Sturgess, Andy Trigg, Geoff Toone, Phil Vesty. The Mercury Walk was the flagship for the club. It generated immense support and spectator-lined routes, pavement deep through the centre of the city, were a brilliant advertisement for walking.

The Novices attracted entries of over 200 and a lot of talent from them flowed into Leicester Walking Club. On the 20 miles course, Charles Keene College lecturer John Sturgess, after speed work on the Abbey Park, in 1977 set the fastest time of 3 hrs 8 mins 59 secs. An obstacle to the development of the event for women was rules restrictions. Distances were limited, but the road running boom opened the law makers' eyes so that eventually women did have a crack at 20. One of them was Doctor Jane Napier of the Royal Infirmary, and the last one before the distance was reduced to 10km was Claire Sharples of Bushby, ex county senior cross country champion.

THE MERCURY WALK

With the exception of World War II and the immediate post war period, the Leicester Mercury Walk has been held continuously since 1927. Its length has been adjusted several times in recent years: to 30 km in 1986, to 20 km in 1990, and to the present 10 km in 1992.

First winner T. Lloyd Johnson won a total of nine Mercury walks, the last occasion being in 1949 in 3-00-07. Other Leicester Walking Club victors are Albert Staines (1939); Pete Markham (1961); Brian Adams (three successive victories between 1977-79; Alan King (1981 and 1982); Simon Moore (1986); and Chris Smith (1993). Eminent winners from elsewhere include Don Thompson (Metropolitan) in 1959 and 1962; Ron Wallwork (Lancs) in 1970; and Daniel Bautista of Mexico in 2-22-53 in 1976. Full details of winners and times are included as an Appendix.

Lunch at the Grand Hotel with the Editor of the Leicester Mercury, and a leisurely ride to the start of the 20 miles race outside Leicester prison in Welford Road, was for many years a time-honoured ritual for the starters. Start was by flag fall, but stopping the traffic to permit the walkers to head towards the city was an honour bound to cease one day as its volume increased.

The Mercury Walk became one of the highlights of the local athletics calendar, and the starters were often a major attraction in themselves. They included distinguished athletes such as Harold Whitlock, 50k walk gold medallist in the 1936 Berlin Olympics (1956), double Olympic silver medallist John Cooper (1965), Melton Olympic swimmer Jean Jeavons (1973), and T. Lloyd Johnson himself (1958 and 1977). Among a long list of other local personalities are Lady Isobel Barnett (1954); Leicester's second female Lord Mayor, Cllr. Mrs Dorothy Russell (1960); Leicester and England goalkeeper Gordon Banks (1966); Colonel Andrew Martin, Lord Lieutenant of Leicestershire for many years (1967); and Palace Theatre variety artist Sam Coster (1955), who entertained the crowd on a three-wheeled bicycle before the race.

LEICESTER TO SKEGNESS - 100 MILES

The east coast town of Skegness has long been a popular resort with Leicester holidaymakers, and in 1958 the Leicester Walking Club, in conjunction with the Skegness publicity unit, arranged the first 100 miles walk between the two. The actual distance being a few miles less, Albert Johnson, who measured the course, put in an extra loop through Scraptoft, continuing on through Uppingham, Peterborough, Market Deeping, Spalding and Boston to finish on the Skegness sea front.

There was a 24 hour time limit, and stragglers were persuaded to come in by car. Cycling attendants accompanied many walkers, dealing with attacks of cramp, and carrying food, liquids and warm clothing for the inevitable drop in temperatures during the night. Mobile vehicles carried supplies, and roll up teams of recorders, timekeepers and judges observed progress and ensured that no one got seriously lost - a Dutch competitor wandered onto a motorway at one point.

Wilf Smith of LWC won the race, but as the Leicester Mercury reported, "it wasn't until three hours later that the Leicester Walking Club knew they had won the team race. The winning team consisted of Smith (1), Albert Staines (9), and Jim Marriott (11),

Not all achievements attract the attention or recognition afforded to the Centurions. In 1967 50-year-old John Sinclair from Leicester walked into Cape Town after a 24 day 1,000 mile trek from Pretoria, only to find that there was no-one there to welcome him. He said his sponsors must have forgotten to tell anyone he was coming. Sinclair was no stranger to non-stop walking. Earlier in 1967, he set a world record by walking 154.25 miles non-stop on Bruntingthorpe Aerodrome in Leicestershire.

but did not include Harold Foreman (7) who was the second Leicester man in. Of the 41 who started, 25 finished, and of these 13 did it for the first time, and so became eligible for election to the Centurion Club. Leicester new Centurions are Smith, Foreman and Albert Tompkinson (13)".

LEICESTER CENTURIONS - THE "TON UP" MEN

A Centurion is one, who as an amateur, has walked in competition, in Great Britain, 100 miles within 24 hours. The Centurions is the most exclusive body in the world. No other organisation demands the same high standards of performance. There are no patrons.

Leicester Walking Club are eminent in this chapter of heel and toe. Their Centurion connection began with Chris Clegg, a World War II soldier serving in the Royal Army Pay Corps, stationed in Leicester. He became Centurion 135 when in 1947 he walked from London Bridge to Brighton and back (104 miles), passing the 100 marker in 21 hrs 39 mins 42 secs. He emigrated to America and returned by invitation in July 1992 to start the bi-annual 100 miles road

Brian Adams (LWC), superb competitor over one to one hundred miles. First British competitor home in the 20k road walk in the 1976 Montreal Olympics. Pictured here at the UK Championships at Crystal Palace in June 1980. (George Herringshaw)

walk from Hungarton village hall in Leicestershire.

Leicester Walking Club have organised 100s every two years since their first to Skegness on July 18 1958. Other routes were later adopted: New Parks School to the Bosworth district and in 1990 and 1992 from Hungarton, one competitor in the latter year being, "Little Mouse" Don Thompson, Rome Olympic champion of 1960. Honours were taken by Sandra Brown and her husband Richard, who finished holding hands, but she had made the pace in the night, especially in the cold, early hours, when retirements are common. Charles Keene College lecturer, John Sturgess, third in 1992, completed the distance on a highly personal diet which included apples and onions.

One 24 hours track race has been held at Saffron Lane, in August 1969. Winner Colin Young (Essex) circled the 440 yards track, 519 times to amass a distance of 129 miles 1,155 yards. Leicester's Mal Blyth came sixth, covering 110 miles 328 yards, and he carried his son on his shoulders around the final lap. But the Leicester club record of 117 miles 594 yards, set by Cyril Evans in 1960, remained unbeaten.

Since 1958 the Dutch have supported Leicester 100's in strength. Their contingent has been organised by Lou Schol, President of the Dutch Centurions. Subsequently the Leicester race became an international event, drawing competitors from all over Europe.

In addition to its first winner Wilf Smith, two other Leicester men have won the Leicester 100, John Heywood, in 1978 and Brian Adams, the only city man to break 18 hours, until joined by world cup walker, Chris Berwick of Leicester Walking Club, who in August 1993 went under 18 in London. Here is Leicester's complete list of the men entitled to wear a Centurions badge, in blue and silver enamel, which bears the seniority number of the holder on a Centurions shield:

		Time	No.			Time	No.
1947	C. Clegg	21 39 42	135	1974	P. Markham	18 46 31	526
1961	C. Evans	20 04 13	158	1974	E. Warner	21 53 36	534
1953	A. Staines	18 50 59	205	1974	W. Roe	22 27 49	538
1953	J. Rawlings	22 07 52	212	1974	C. Rushton	22 43 11	539
1955	T. Sharlott	20 12 53	236	1974	R. Morris	23 43 21	546
1956	J. Marriott	21 32 57	265	1976	D. Palfreman	20 25 59	587
1958	W. Smith	18 02 37	275	1976	M. Loach	22 23 52	591
1958	H. Foreman	19 53 52	279	1976	U. Limbert	23 33 52	597
1958	A. Tompkinson	22 03 57	280	1978	J. Heywood	18 19 00	627
1958	E. Leech	22 38 52	283	1978	A. Kent	22 44 56	636
1960	A. Cooper	21 41 47	306	1980	C. Bent	20 39 17	694
1960	A. Kirkpatrick	22 35 06	311	1980	D. Wilkinson	22 14 07	702
1960	L. Matthews	23 40 45	316	1980	E. Macdermid	23 22 25	711
1964	J. Leech	21 26 47	358	1982	R. Storer	19 26 43	720
1966	M. Blyth	20 26 15	384	1984	B. Adams	17 39 28	778
1966	J. Nutt	20 34 44	385	1986	A. Thacker	21 50 24	805
1966	D. Pook	22 20 05	394	1986	P. Baxter	22 34 37	806
1966	R. Stapleford	22 52 34	401	1988	J. Sturgess	19 15 58	829
1968	D. Trigg	22 20 42	422	1993	C. Berwick	17 57 07	902
1968	D. Malyon	23 11 01	425				
1970	D. Jones	23 03 25	458				

5 ROAD RUNNING

Interest in road running expanded rapidly following the first London marathon in 1981. It was almost like putting the clock back a 100 years to the period when so many clubs were of the harrier type only, and did not cater for track and field. In 1928, however, Mr S.H.B. Livingston, a director of city firm of shoe machinery merchants, Livingston and Doughty, presented a cup for an annual road relay race, restricted by invitation to Midland clubs. It was originally from the County Cricket ground, Aylestone Road, into the county and back via Blaby, Cosby, Whetstone and Enderby, a distance of 21 miles.

LIVINGSTON ROAD RELAY

A feature of the early running of the event was that Mr Livingston provided a chauffeur driven Rolls Royce to assist with the organisation and to carry officials and friends around the Avenue Road Extension course. Afterwards all competitors and officials sat down to a free tea, and the cup and prizes were presented.

In 1940, petrol rationing and essential war time uses only forced a change to a start in Avenue Road Extension, Leicester. The lap distance was 3 miles and 45 yards with five runners per team. It stayed like that until 1975 when a slight alteration was made, making the lap 3 miles and 153 yards. Traffic congestion influenced a move of starting point into Greenhill Road. However, a year later, in the interests of safety, it was moved out of the city to Holwell Works, Asfordby Hill, near Melton Mowbray. Messrs Stanton and Stavely gave permission for the use of their excellent premises with full use of their miners- type bathing and shower facilities. Lap distance was 3³/₄ miles, established by Leicester Coritanian Cliff Baguley, a local resident and an employee of Pace Consultants Leicester, who had already put on their own relay event. Changeovers were all inside the works premises on traffic free roads and the lap was instantly improved. Subsequently National and Midland relay championships were held on it.

After 1940 the race developed to be one of the best known and occupied a senior reputation in the Midlands. It has been held every year since its inception, except for 1979, when 12 feet high snow drifts in Welby Lane caused a cancellation. The 66th year of the event in 1993 was celebrated from the Mine, Asfordby, when Leicester Coritanians won for the fourth time in five years. However, a local club did not win this high quality test until 1949, when Leicester Harriers recorded their only success in the race. The team was Jack Driver (15-23), Allan Lewis (16-04), Phil Driver (16-47), George Waller (16-40), John Honour (16-19). Some 17 years later, Leicester Colleges of Art and Technology notched a lone success and their total time of 72-11, compared with Leicester Harriers 81-13, underlined rising standards. Art and Tech were represented by: Phil Lancaster (14-17), Pete Bourne (14-52), John Eccleston (14-37), John Offord (14-33), Ron Grove (13-52).

Leicester Coritanians first win in 1989 came via Tony Walker (18-24), Kevin O'Neill (18-28), Phil Makepeace (18-14), John Grindey (18-08), Joey Masterson (18-17). A year later Coritanians winning combination was: Steve Needs (18-41), Kevin O'Neill (18-32), Rob Sheen (18-58), Alan Maddocks (18-32), Dave Lem Junior (19-03). The third success came in 1992 with Nigel Stirk leading off for an inaugural lap record of 18-59 from the

Mine, followed by Andy Hart (19-29), Kevin O'Neill (19-02), Rob Sheen (19-36), Pete Davies (19-11). In March 1993, Stirk took lap one in 18-54 and then Needs ran 19-25, Maddocks 19-18, Masterson 19-01 and Hart 19-38.

HALT! WHO GOES THERE?

A gleaming Rolls Royce was stopped at the gates of the English Electric premises, Whetstone, Leicestershire, venue for the inaugural AAA National 12-man road relay championship in 1967. Devoid of an official car park sticker, the owner, reclining nonchalantly in the rear seat, was informed he couldn't enter. The chauffeur was despatched to get one, and in the meantime an amicable conversation flowed between the gatekeeper for the day, Ted Johnson (father of Olympian Ken) and the occupant. Ted was praised for doing his job zealously and when the pass was produced noted the car number and name of the visitor. It was AAA 1 and it belonged to the President of the Amateur Athletic Association, the Most Hon. The Marquess of Exeter, K.C.M.G., LLD.

From 1976 to 1984 there were no problems. But in 1983 strange oil like drilling rigs appeared on nearby land the first probings for coal. Several years earlier there had been rumours of there being big coal deposits and the truth came on with a rush, when something more substantial than drilling began to get underway. In 1985, a move was made to the Gartree Prison, Market Harborough by permission of Governor, Richard Stilt. The lap was five kilometres and there was a lot of co-operation on the spot for the next four years. Harborough AC had a big input and Stuart Harrison of the prison staff provided immense support.

In 1989, the Asfordby Mine was opened and permission was given to move back to the old circuit, which although having some differences was almost the same. Stilton Striders, the local athletic club, took over the reins, putting the race on annually with the remeasured distance being 3.8 miles.

Of the 64 races to date, Derby and County AC have the proudest record with 20 victories. Coventry Godiva Harriers trail them with 15, Tipton Harriers 14, Birchfield Harriers 4, Coritanians 4, Small Heath 3, Sheffield Harriers 3, Leicester Harriers 1, Art and Tech 1. Scores of internationals and champions have turned out in the Livingston, making it a great event of the past with a lot still going for it in the future.

Samuel Henry Bias Livingston himself was President of Leicestershire and Rutland AAA from 1934 - 1964, and also President of Leicestershire County Cricket Club for some years.

LIVINGSTON ROAD RELAY PROGRESSIVE COURSE AND LAP RECORDS

COURSE RECORDS

From Avenue Road Extension Leicester.
Lap of 3 miles 45 yards (X5).

1943	Coventry	81-22
1945	Derby	80-14
1946	Small Heath	78-53
1947	Coventry	78-48
1948	Coventry	78-03
1951	Coventry	77-51
1952	Derby	77-39
1953	Birchfield	75-08
1955	Birchfield	74-55
1957	Small Heath	74-21
1959	Birchfield	73-57
1960	Derby	73-01
1963	Coventry	71-42
1968	Coventry	70-02

Start Greenhill Road. Lap 3 miles 153 yards

1975	Tipton	72-49

Move to Asfordby. Lap 3³/₄ miles

1976	Birchfield	89-45
1977	Tipton	88-45
1978	Tipton	88-26
1983	Derby	87-48

Move to Gartree Prison. Lap 5 km.

1985	Tipton	74-45
1986	Sheffield	74-17
1987	Sheffield	74-09

Move to Asfordby Hill, Holwell Works.
Lap 6 km.

1989	Coritanians	91-31
1991	Tipton	91-02

Move to The Mine, Asfordby. Lap 3.8 miles

1992	Coritanians	96-14
1993	Coritanians	96-10

LAP RECORDS

3 miles 45 yards

1940	D. Harman	Tipton	15-19
1946	J. Holden	Tipton	14-53
1953	E. Hardy	Derby	14-32
1954	E. Hardy	Derby	14-30
1957	A. Keily	Derby	14-29
1959	A. Keily	Derby	14-28
1960	K. Johnson	LCAT	14.24
1961	M. Bullivant	Derby	14-10
1963	B. Kilby	Coventry	14-06
1966	R. Grove	LCAT	13-52
1967	R. Taylor	Coventry	13-43
1968	R. Taylor	Coventry	13-43

3 miles 153 yards

1970	D. Lem	Birchfield	13-38
1975	D. Black	Small Heath	13-29

3.8 miles

1976	I. Stewart	Birchfield	16-57
1978	I. Stewart	Tipton	16-51

5 Kilometres

1985	T. Milovsorov	Tipton	14-20

6 Kilometres

1989	D. Long	Massey Ferguson	17-28

3.8 miles

1992	N. Stirk	Coritanians	18-59
1993	R. Hollingsworth	Notts	18-08

* 1979 In the Pace Road Relay, Nick Rose (Bristol), twice English cross country champion, ran 16-33 on the 3.8 mile lap.
*1983 Mike McLeod (Morpeth) Olympic silver medallist, ran fastest ever of 16-31 in AAA Championship.

"LET'S FORM A ROAD RUNNING LEAGUE"

In 1983, Leicester Coritanian Ted Toft originated the proposal of forming a road running league as interest expanded after the first London marathon with the formation of new city and county clubs.

Ted advocated the adopting of existing road races and from this limpet operation worked out a points scoring system to determine individual and team champions. Sponsored by the Leicester Runner, a sports goods shop in Rutland, later Granby Street (Prop, Coritanian Tony Walker), the league chose seven events. They were April 15, Rutland Water mini marathon; May 30, Gartree 5; June 26, Wigston 7; July 22, Ascot 10km; August 19, GEC 10; September 2, Enderby 6; October 14, Bellshire half marathon.

The first season results were:

MEN	Pts		LADIES	Pts
1 Oadby and Wigston Legionnaires	27,119		1 Huncote Harriers	4070
2 Leicester Coritanians	26,513		2 Oadby and Wigston Legionnaires	3448
3 Stilton Striders AC	26,103		3 Braunstone Town Joggers	3012
4 GEC Harriers	25,978		4 Stilton Striders	2727
5 Coalville Harriers	25,763		5 Charnwood AC	2354
6 Huncote Harriers	24,746		6 Leicester Coritanians	1733

VETERANS (MEN) (40 plus)	Pts
1 GEC Harriers	4055
2 Coalville Harriers	4031
3 Oadby and Wigston Legionnaires	4006
4 Leicester Coritanians	3999
5 Bowline Climbing Club	3730
6 Charnwood AC	3314

INDIVIDUAL CHAMPION Mick Strange (Owls)

Other clubs competing in the League were Wreake Runners, Leicestershire County Council and Leicester University.

LEICESTER CHARITIES MARATHON

The Charities' day of sport started on September 23 1979 as a marathon jog of 26 miles 385 yards from Victoria Park, as part of Lord Mayor Cllr. Albert S. Watson's X-Ray Scanner Appeal. It was sponsored by Castles Motors, Churchgate, Leicester and organised by MD, Iain Davidson, a trained athlete himself.

There was an immediate cheque of £5,000 handed over to the appeal, and over 400 took part. The route was two and a half times round the park, out on the Welford Road to Wigston, Oadby Road, Wigston, Brabazon Road, Race Course Drive, Ring Road, Shanklin Drive and London Road and back to Victoria Park, which is ten miles, and then two more laps of eight miles each.

Joint winners of the first event in 1979 were John Alcock, Bob King and Chris Smith, all of Leicester Coritanians, in 2-38-16. First home among the women was Gillian Bottoms of Charnwood AC in 3-34-30. Leicester Coritanians, through its secretary, Ted Toft actively helped organise and marshal the event.

Various charities later benefited and thousands ran for their own individual cause. A million pounds bonanza may have accrued by 1994. One special cause well remembered was Project 81. Mrs Patricia Corah was chairman and funds were raised for a Leicestershire Association for the Disabled holiday bungalow. T-shirts were produced, overprinted "Project 81" and the Olympic gold medallist Sebastian Coe lent his support. Nearly two months before the date of the marathon, entries had reached 1,300.

After the popularity of marathon running changed to shorter distances, Leicester followed suit and when Leicester became Britain's first Environment City in 1990, the Charities Marathon was re-named the Great Green Run. Now based on Abbey Park, over 10,000m, solid support continues to provide money for good causes.

COUNTY MARATHON RECORD HOLDER

Several local athletes have excelled as marathon runners, foremost among them the county marathon record holder John Offord.

John has a marvellous video recording of the race at Maasluis, Holland in April 1984 in which he set a County marathon record of 2 hrs. 13 mins. 52 secs. Currently of Beaumont Leys Athletic Club, he has been a member of many clubs including Coritanians and the Owls. Born on 3 April 1947, as a youth he won the Midland cross country championship, has won steeplechase honours and is the county record holder for the 3,000m event with 8 mins. 43.8 secs. at Crystal Palace in 1973.

A. R. Mills (Leicester Harriers),
winner of the Polytechnic Marathon
1920-22. He also competed in the
marathon in the Olympic Games in
Antwerp in 1920 and in Paris in 1924.
(T .J. Sharlott)

He also ran for City Boys School, Leicester Art and Tech, and when working in London, Herne Hill Harriers. A great supporter of local events, he is still running brilliantly as a veteran, looking back on globe-trotting experiences in the marathon, particularly in Berlin, Hong Kong and Penang.

In a famous back to back, he added his prestige to the Leicester marathon, winning in 2-26-48, and seven days later, though he had obviously jeopardised his chances by running in the city, ran an amazing 2-28-47, in Berlin. Over shorter distances he has clocked 48-34 for 10 miles at Michelin, and again supporting local races, has competed in the Leicester Mercury 20 miles road walk.

"ULTRAS"

A handful of athletes have competed across the ultra distance of 100 km - 62 miles 242 yards. The 100 km was featured in the first AAA championship to include Welsh status at Holme Pierrepoint, Nottingham, in May 1989.

Among the competitors was the Welsh international Trevor Hawes of Leicestershire County Council AC, already a veteran of 54 marathons. An unorthodox stylist, whose contortions defy all known mechanical principles of economic running, Trevor has time and again churned out eye catching performances. He had won two marathons in Malta and Barcelona in hot conditions and in his preparation had included six 30 mile runs.

Trevor won in a superb 6 hr. 43 min. 55 sec.

Aged 33, he had suffered extensive blistering but finished eight and a half minutes in front of the field, and at the end of the first of 21 laps, was nearly half a minute in front. Recognised as a championship best performance, his stature rocketed overnight, and with 100km being increasingly recognised at international level he would be an automatic choice. Over the marathon distance of 26.2. miles, Hawes was a regular winner of the Robin Hood, Nottingham, his best being 2-22-20. In 1983, however, Trevor ran his career best of 2-17-33. A man with a fast recovery rate, six weeks after the 100k, he won the Sheffield marathon for the sixth time.

1993 The Pace Consultants road relay race celebrated its 22nd birthday, at the Coalmine, Asfordby Hill, near Melton. Financed, encouraged and with direct aid on the day, it has played a primary role in the road running affairs of the county, thanks to the Director, Tony Hopkins. It has been won seven times by Leicester Coritanians.

Across city and county Hilary Johnson of Harborough AC, mother of Tigers' International Martin, is highly respected as the long serving county schools team manager, and Britain's ultra team manager. As an enormously experienced long distance runner, Hilary can rub shoulders with any in the world ultra fraternity. Winner of the Leicester Charities marathon four times on Victoria Park, she once won an age category in the London, but did not know until months afterwards when reading an athletics magazine. She was an All-England schools competitor over 800m, and also put the shot.

En route to tackling 100km, Hilary won the GEC Whetstone 20 miles in 2-15-28 and the 36 miler, Two Bridges Rosyth in a record 4-15-23. Jumping the months after running the Lincoln-Grantham 100k, Hilary ran a brilliant 19th for Britain in Italy in a World Cup Ultra distance race at the age of 46. At her best she ran 8½ hours.

Over a mountainous course from Florence to Faenza - 4000 feet of ascent - against the best, Britain finished third to Germany and Russia. Much of the race took place in darkness causing navigation problems. After many rough patches, Hilary finished in 9 hours 54 minutes. Trevor Hawes should have been in that race, but a hip injury prevented him from competing.

6 SCHOOLS ATHLETICS

From the later 19th century, many athletics activities centred on youth organisations or churches and chapels. Typical of the latter was the Horseshoe Athletics Club, originally formed by half a dozen young men at Robert Hall Memorial Church on Narborough Road. In addition many schools held their own sports days or athletics meetings.Just beyond Leicester, one of the most prestigious was the annual fixture of Long Street Elementary School in Wigston Magna. Inaugurated in 1922, the meeting was regularly attended by large crowds. The school was later to provide Leicestershire Schools AA with its longest serving secretary, Hylton Herrick, from 1931-60.

CITY SCHOOLS OPT OUT OF NEW SCHOOLS AA

There was no lack of support for athletics in the city schools. However, at a meeting in the Turkey Cafe in Granby Street on February 23 1927, Leicester teachers decided not to join a proposed Leicestershire Schools Athletic Association, thus depriving hundreds of young local athletes of an opportunity to represent their county in the English Schools Championships.

The National Schools athletic body, founded in 1925, organised the championships. In anticipation of an approach to join being made, there had been discussions in recent months, led by Arthur Capers, with colleagues at football matches. Principals in these tasks were Capers (Enderby CoE), Frank Roberts (Kegworth), Frank Rhodes (Church School, Market Harborough), and Bill Reynolds (Melton Council School). Among their ideas was the division of the county into a number of administrative and competitive areas. They proposed a duplication of football and athletic boundaries and these were adopted.

At this time in 1927, there was in existence a Leicester City Athletic Association who were running their own annual championships. Their representatives decided they would not join the new body, fearful, perhaps, of diluting their own autonomy. However, it was left open for them to join later, as it was to all other schools or schools associations who were not represented. The honour of serving as the first President went to Sir Arthur Hazlerigg. Areas were to pay subscriptions of ten shillings (50p) a year and schools one shilling (5p). The first Leicestershire Schools Athletic Championships took place only two weeks before the All England. This historic event graced the Corinthians football ground in Brown's Lane, Loughborough.

**Leicester Coritanians' brilliant discus thrower Karen Mallard, believing that she had the potential to set an age record, came very close to doing that in a competitive trial at the Saffron Lane Sports Centre on April 16, 1974.
Aged 16, Karen heaved the discus 43.18m but it was 1.20m short of the figures set by a C. Chalk in 1971.**

The events were almost in line with the prevailing All England programme, although boys events differed slightly. The half mile or 880 yards was not included, but the girls programme was exactly the same as that detailed in the first national championships.

Rules for the All England allowed each county association to nominate three competitors. Two would take part in the 100 and 220 yards for boys, and 100 and 150 yards for girls. In other events they would nominate two and compete one, but associations were under no obligation to contest all events. All competitors had to be under 14 years of age on March 31 in the current year of competition.

FIRST LEICESTERSHIRE SCHOOLS AA SPORTS

The first Leicestershire Schools AA sports were held at Loughborough on June 25 1927, and "although the Association was only founded in February", the **Leicester Evening Mail** *reported, "the existence of an excellent organising committee has secured for the county schools the privilege of sending representatives to Stamford Bridge on July 16 when the junior Inter County Championships will be held".*

Teams from North Leicestershire, Loughborough, Market Harborough, Mid Leicestershire and Melton Mowbray competed. Performances were modest by comparison with those of the first English Schools Championships at Crystal Palace in 1925, and Leicestershire clearly had some way to go to challenge for awards. However, county schools were now in a position to name their first representatives to the third All England championships. This proved to be a baptism of fire. Not one local athlete was good enough to get into the top three, but eyes had been opened, lessons learned.

 Comparing the 1927 results with those of the inaugural meeting of 1925, it showed that standards had rocketed and that it was southern counties who were the most powerful. The cinder track at Stamford Bridge hosted many top class meetings and might have been in superior condition to the old circuit in the Crystal Palace grounds. However, any difference between the two could not possibly account for the big difference in times. The boys 880 yards in 1927 was 12 seconds faster than in 1925 and in the girls 440 yards relay, time returned was nine seconds quicker.

Undoubtedly the general improvement had come about then, as it does today, with a harder training and more of it, and careful planning in loading the schedule and racing. Possibly more Southern counties teachers were in direct contact with athletic clubs and as standards there were considerably higher than in Leicestershire, their knowledge of the art of coaching would be more advanced.

The Schools Athletic Association, recognising the need to help and advise in backward areas, began publishing instructional booklets and the first one appeared in 1928. Many books were published and those purporting to point the way to athletic success were most popular. A familiar name then and more recently repeated on the cinema screen, in the *Chariots of Fire* film, was that of Sam Mussabini, trainer of Harold Abrahams, the 1924 Olympic 100 metres champion. Mussabini wrote a bible for his time, the *Complete Athletic Trainer* first published in 1913. Subsequently small booklets under his name were sold and in the 30's they could be obtained from the well known shop "Sports" in Belvoir Street, Leicester.

ALFRED ADCOCK - LEICESTERSHIRE'S FIRST ALL ENGLAND CHAMPION

Alfred Adcock, a talented athlete attending the Old British School, King Street, Melton Mowbray won the Boys' Under 14 long jump at Reading in 1931 with a distance of 16ft. 5in. (5m.). His parents were from Leicester, and kept the Dixie Arms in the city before moving to Asfordby, near Melton.

Alfred Adcock of Asfordby, Leicestershire's first All England champion. He won the Boys' Under 14 long jump in 1931 with a distance of 16ft 5in (5m). (George Herringshaw)

Alfred started his education at the Church of England School, Main Street, Asfordby. He jumped streams which were too wide for others to try and was said to run like the wind.

When he moved to a senior school in Melton, he would walk the two miles from village to town and back, twice a day. He developed leg strength, and before going to Reading to represent Leicestershire Schools broke the national record in the county championship, set by J. Tomkins (Middlesex) with a leap of 17ft 8½in. (5.40m.) at Stamford Bridge in 1929.

Between that performance and going to the All England, the *Leicester Mercury* reported that: "A.R. Adcock, the Melton Schoolboy who broke the national long jump record for schoolboys at the Leicester Schools meeting at Wigston, jumped the remarkable distance of 18 feet, whilst practising on the School's Sports Ground yesterday."

On leaving school, Alfred Adcock proudly retained a certificate presented to him by Leicestershire Schools Athletic Association when winning the long jump title at the county sports in 1931, the only thing that remained to remind him of his prowess. Alfred died in February 1984 at the age of 66.

Footnote: In the E.S.A.A. Standards Tables for 1989, a district standard long jump for boys under 14 is given as 4.65m. (15ft. 3in.). His best performance of 18 feet, aged 13, would have won, with the exception of M. Vickery's (Northants 19ft. 2 1/2ins.) of 1933, all the national titles from 1925 to 1948. That helps put into perspective the rare talent of Alfred Adcock over half a century ago.

PRIMARY SCHOOLS CROSS COUNTRY LEAGUE

The Leicestershire Primary Schools cross country league is a success story that is set to run for a long time. It was founded in 1977 by teacher Rob Osborn, who circulated a letter asking "Are you interested?" In response 327 boys and girls turned up at Kirby Muxloe Primary School. Boys ran two miles and girls 1½ over a parkland course suitable for wearing spikes. Inaugural winners were Ian Martin (Countesthorpe) with Ravenhurst the top team. For the girls, Hazel Lewitt of Ravenhurst was the first home, and her school also won the team race and went through the season unbeaten.

Venues varied in future years but no one could have anticipated the way the league would grow, eventually involving up to a hundred schools in city and county. Such numbers generated mass support. On Saturday mornings, cross country fever caused traffic jams. Mobile parents raced from one point to another urging on their offspring and their school teams at the same time. To exert adequate control over the masses of spectators and children, the City Council was approached for permission for the use Western and Braunstone Parks. These have hosted numerous Inter-Counties, national and All-England events and are consequently well known to the UK running fraternity.

Four meetings are held monthly from September to December, and at the end of the 1992 campaign another record number of boys and girls had taken part. Figures were Minor girls 957; Minor boys 1884; Major girls 1115; Major boys 1756; Total 5712.

The claim that this is probably the biggest league of its kind in the country has never been challenged. Runners come in all shapes and sizes and various levels of fitness, and obtain experience of starting in big fields, preparing for the ultimate test in years to come of qualifying for a county place in the English Schools Championships. Since October 1977, many well known runners have gone on to achieve the highest possible recognition. Several have expressed the debt they owe to the league, but they have also, as so many do, stressed the importance of representing their own school - an honour that might not have been possible to obtain in other sports.

Two national women's cross country champions started in the league, Leicester Coritanians Lisa York and Helen Titterington. Helen in 1988 was the youngest national cross country champion for 37 years. In her first 10,000m on the track, she finished fourth in the World Students Games in a superb 33-39 and also lifted the national 10km road title.

Lisa York won the first cross country trial for world juniors in 1989 and reached the top of the winter sport on Cheltenham racecourse in a scintillating national victory in 1992. She has run in the world championships, set an All-Comers one mile indoors record in the National Indoor Arena Birmingham, has a fastest lap world relay plaque and qualified for the Barcelona Olympic Games by a power winning display in the WAA 3000 metres. Like Leicester Coritanian clubmate Maxine Newman, both were coached by John Price at critical phases of their careers.

A secret of the success of the league must be its different category awards, based on schools

Helen Titterington (LC). One of the youngest athletes ever to win a national cross country title, and a superb 10k track competitor. (George Herringshaw)

populations. At the end of the season, large, medium, small and high schools for example are all eligible for team trophies. There is an enormous amount of work involved and some 20 A4 sheets are required to give the detail of what has happened in each race. Currently, Rod Essex processes the mass of paperwork and circulates the results. An enthusiastic committee oil vital administration, with cross country secretaries Madeline Robins and Christine Parker at the centre of affairs.

By the 1920s, athletics was a major spectator sport. Crowds of 20,000 were not unusual at major events, but until the 1960s Leicester had no facilities adequate to attract top class meetings. In 1924, the plight of athletes was summed up in the Sports Mercury. "I am sorry to say boys that there will be no cinder track for you this summer... several junior athletes living near the Spinney Hill Park have been threatened with all sorts of penalties if they persist in running in the park". In September, Fred Cox visited Battersea Park, London where the facilities made him "seethe with vexatious envy. Oh for some lion hearted sportsman who will provide us with a track - then, not till then, will Leicester be enrolled on the championship records."

In the nineteenth century finding **anywhere** to compete was at times a problem. The Wharf Street Cricket Ground, opened in 1825, was used for sports as well as balloon ascents, firework displays, public dinners and cricket itself. However this was sold for building in 1860, just as organised athletics was beginning to take off in Leicester. With the closure of Wharf Street, cricket and other sports including professional sprinting transferred to the Racecourse, now Victoria Park. It was not until 1878 that a purpose built cycling and running track became available at the Aylestone Ground of the Leicestershire Cricket Ground Company on what is now Grace Road.

AYLESTONE CRICKET GROUND

The ground, covering 12 acres of land formerly belonging to the Duke of Rutland, had a cinder track around its perimeter probably extending for 500 yards, or three laps to the mile. The programme of the first athletics meeting held there is in the archives of Leicestershire County Cricket Club, of which Mr E.E. Snow, author of a history of county cricket, is the custodian.

This is the oldest known surviving athletics programme in the county. It relates to the Leicester Athletic Society's eighth annual sports on July 8 1878 and suggests that significant changes had taken place in the years since the Society's formation. There is distinguished patronage, under the Duke of Rutland, Lord John Manners MP, Colonel Frederick Burnaby of Somerby Hall, T.T. Paget Esq, J.D. Harris, and the Mayor C. Stretton Esq. Grace Road later became the sports ground of the City of Leicester School, and after 1946, the permanent home of Leicestershire County Cricket Club.

BELGRAVE ROAD GROUND

A second sports ground was opened on the west side of Belgrave Road in 1880. Covering around 10 acres, this too was encircled by a cycling and running track. It was a relatively short-lived venture, and in 1901 part of the British Shoe Machinery Company's works was built on the site.

The Belgrave Road Cricket and Bicycle Grounds were opened on Saturday May 15 1880 by Colonel Burnaby, Lord of the Manor of Somerby, and a patron of athletics in Leicestershire, who arrived with his wife in a carriage drawn by a pair of greys. Principal partners in the enterprise were Mr Billson, the rope merchant of Belgrave Gate, whose former premises opposite Abbey Street carried his name until a few years ago; Mr Illesley, landlord of the Black Lion, Belgrave Gate; and a Mr Newton who negotiated a 13 years lease of the land with the owner, George Harrison.

The trotting track had a width of 25 feet and three laps to the mile. Inside this was the bicycle course and athletics track, 440 yards on the inside lane or four laps to the mile. For sprint races a track 200 yards long was expected to be "exceedingly useful." A stand capable of holding 3000 people was planned and also a gymnasium.

The inaugural meeting lasted three days and included athletics, cycling and pony trotting. On Monday, the second day, there were over ten thousand people present. Harry Hutchens of Putney, the famous London professional sprinter was the star attraction. Later in his career, Hutchens was a key figure in the riots at Lillie Bridge, London, where stands were burnt to the ground - he being involved in a bookmakers' fiddle. At Belgrave Road, Hutchens ran in the 120 yards handicap for a first prize of

Tom Barratt (NGTE), prolific winner of Midland field event titles, pictured at the 1949 Midland Championships. The judge in the background is Bob Wight, Leicester University athletics supremo. (George Herringshaw)

£20. He was the backmarker in the handicap, having to give 25 yards start to W. Lambert, and he failed to get up. The referee and timekeeper for the meeting was Mr G.W. Atkinson, of the *Sporting Life*, a sheet still catering for the horse racing and gambling fraternity.

The Colonel in his opening address had expressed a wish "that the grounds be honestly conducted and all races fairly and pleasantly fought." It was clear what he had in mind for in one of the professional sprints there was an objection to the winner, on the ground that he was "Not the Greensmith he had represented himself to be." Clearly, the ugly head of impersonation had already reared itself.

The Belgrave Road ground flourished for several years, and handicap meetings on summer evenings and Saturdays were held regularly. Leicester Football Club - the Tigers - played on the Belgrave Road Ground in their first season in 1880, and Leicester Fosse F.C. also played there in 1887-88. Inter club races over road and nearby country were run from the ground, and on the cycling side at Belgrave Road, there were many international challenge matches.

Colonel Burnaby, a staunch patron and supporter of Leicestershire athletics, was killed on January 17 1885, only five years after opening Belgrave Road, at the battle of Abou Klea, struck by a javelin which severed his jugular vein.

MANOR ROAD

Several athletic clubs and business organisations had their own grounds: Wolsey at Aylestone, the BU at Mowmacre Hill and the Police Recreation Ground on Melton Road, shared until the 1960s by the Belgrave United Athletic Club. In May 1951, however, there began a most harmonious and productive relationship between Leicester University lecturer Bob Wight and the Leicestershire and Rutland AAA. In 1950, no county championships were held because of ground difficulties. In that year En-tout-cas laid down a cinder track for the University at Manor Road, Oadby. Sympathetic to the plight of the AAA, Bob Wight invited the County to hold their annual championships at Manor Road in May 1951. They stayed at Manor Road until the opening of the new synthetic track at the Sports Centre, Saffron Lane, in 1967.

There was an expansion of other track and field activities against a backcloth and surroundings of immaculate grass areas, a small wood, packed with bluebells, snowdrops and other wild flowers. Girded by hedges and flanked by numerous trees, many regarded the place as idyllic compared with the urban, concrete architecture of Saffron Lane. Leicestershire clubs competed at Manor Road regularly against the University at the start of the season and were invited as special team representatives against quality opposition. Tubingen University, Germany, sent teams, and other Colleges came to spice competition.

University Athletics Union (UAU) Championships, including pentathlons and decathlons and Midland men and women's championships, were held and superbly organised by Bob Wight. Athletes who became famous ran there whilst in their

Leicester University's much admired track at Manor Road in the early 1960s. The event is the Inter County mile, and the competitors are 2 Maurice Herriott, GB steeplechaser, 3 Dave Lem, and 5 Pete Blakesley, LC mile champion. (Bob Newton)

apprentice days at University. Among them was John Whetton (Manchester U), a European 1500m winner and Ron Hill, a Whetton team mate, a former World 10-mile record holder, who is highly regarded for the work he did on perfecting the 'Diet' for marathon athletes.

University student David Littlewood has chaired the AAA rules revision committee, was Referee at the World Students Games in Sheffield and is currently the Secretary of the English Schools Athletic Association. The Leicester Tigers player Tom Bleasedale was a leading county shot putter whilst at LU. A brilliant all-rounder was Jacqueline Taylor, the UAU pentathlon champion.

Bob Wight organised courses for officials, resulting in a stream of men and women being made available to help at local and, eventually, at national meetings. Bob was an authority on the Olympic movement, and his favourite film, *The Berlin Olympics*, was shown at the beginning of each year to new University students. Meticulous records were kept of all University and visiting athletes at Manor Road, but in 1967, with the Saffron Lane operation about to begin, the end of the halcyon period at Manor Road was in sight.

When it came a "Thanks Varsity for the Manor! was penned in the *Leicester Sports Mercury*:

"...now is the time to thank Leicester University for their holding operation which began 16 years ago. Town and Gown were hardly acquainted with each other in those days, but in the ensuing period many knots of friendship were tied and there developed an association which has benefited local athletics.

"It is not possible to measure the gains from athletes being permitted to train at the University Ground, Manor Road, or to compute the number of occasions when stirring contests have left spectator and competitor vibrating with excitement. Since 1951 the main County AAA championship meeting has been staged at Manor Road, a fact which alone will account for past and present champions having a particular happy memory of the Manor.

"The championships, although a highlight in any season, represent a fraction of local fixtures. Matches between the University and County clubs will go on as before - some at Manor Road and clubs now able to invite the students to Saffron Lane for the return engagements. The University will continue to present their own top attractions such as British Universities championships and the WIVAB (Womens Inter Varsity Athletics Board) match in which Leicestershire Girls have been accustomed to a competitive sting, seldom experienced in club affairs."

In recognition of the vital role played by Bob Wight, he was honoured with a County AAA Life Vice Presidency.

FIRST COUNTY CHAMPIONSHIPS AT MANOR ROAD

In the first county championships at Manor Road on June 2 1951, no fewer than eight championship best performances were recorded.

Among them were Ken Johnson (LCAT) winner of the mile in 4-25, who a year later ran in the Helsinki Olympic Games steeplechase. Don Cobley (Hinckley Technical College and RAF), a county swimming and senior cross country champion triumphed in the three miles. His all-round ability which included horse riding, pistol shooting and fencing enabled him to win two British Modern Pentathlon titles and he competed in two Olympic Games in 1956 in Melbourne and 1960 in Rome. Junior Matthew Dodds of Ashby GS excelled in high hurdles and discus and his highly specialised skills in several other events were ultimately proven with him later winning the AAA Decathlon championship.

The 120 yards hurdles final was cancelled when only one competitor, R. Bailey of LCAT, turned up. He "sportingly refused to accept the championship". In the women's events, a new record was established in the 100 yards by Miss J. Giblet of Leicester

Harriers in 11.3 seconds.

Other Manor Road meetings of immense interest include the visit of Tubingen University (Germany) in 1960. On a cold night, the Germans beat Leicester University and a County AAA team. In the same year, English, Scottish Universities and the County clashed in a triangular match and inter city athletics between Leicester-Derby-Nottingham were another big highlight of 1960.

More recently in the late 80's, a new generation of mainly road runners have relished running on the Manor Road cinders in meetings arranged by Huncote Harriers. Indispensable to such gatherings was the head groundsman, Mr S. Cadle, one of the few remaining highly respected experts who possess the know how of marking out a blank cinder track, complete with eight lanes and all intermediary markings.

SAFFRON LANE SPORTS CENTRE

A grass track facility for athletes and cyclists was provided in 1952 by the city council at Saffron Lane. Pre-war it had been the Agricultural Showground and had the remains of a wooden grandstand which was declared unsafe and had to be demolished. During the war an underground shelter had been built on there, and other concrete fortifications for use by the army.

The city's long awaited purpose built stadium was slow to materialise. "For more that 10 years Leicester City Council has been talking of it's plans..........", wrote the *Illustrated Leicester Chronicle* in January 1954, but a project planned for Aylestone Meadows was "too costly to carry out...........Time and again plans have been blocked by shortage of money". Alderman Wale, chairman of the parks committee, also took a pessimistic view saying "I doubt if I'll be alive when it is done". More than 13 years were to pass before plans came to reality. In the meantime, the Aylestone Meadows scheme had been abandoned, and the new sports centre was built on the Saffron Lane ground itself.

The superb all-weather track - a "K" surface - was the centrepiece of the Saffron Lane Sports Centre, opened by Her Royal Highness, the Duchess of Gloucester on May 6 1967. Over 40 years of campaigning for a public track were at last at an end. "For the first time in the history of the City there will be adequate facilities for organised sport and recreation", said Lord Mayor Monica Trotter of the completion of the first phase of Saffron Lane. In the opinion of Chairman of the Parks Committee, Ald. F.J. Jackson JP, the stadium would raise the standard of athletics both locally and nationally, and "will result in this country achieving even better results in international competition".

The Centre had separate tracks for athletics and cycling. The athletics track - four laps to the mile - was laid out to international standards to enable the submission of records for ratification. The programme for the opening day included a Ladies Hockey Match in the cycling arena between Leicestershire and a Midlands XI. During the hockey match interval there was to be an eight laps point to point on the new cycling track, 333 and one third metres of mastic asphalt, but unfortunately the weather broke, and heavy rain and winds interfered so much with the cycling programme that much of it had to be abandoned.

"This is a fabulous track" was the description given to the 440 yards track and field events runways by Olympic long jump champion, Lynn Davies. Sports Centre manager, Brian Kilby, the European and Commonwealth Games marathon champion, was to remember that quote which was reinforced by many internationals taking part in the match - North, V South, V Midlands and Wales.

The *Leicester Mercury* report appeared under the headline "Long jumper Lynn wants to return...Athletic performances suffered by rain-affected tracks at many meetings in England on Saturday, but not on the all-weather surface at Leicester Sports Centre, which received a cascade of compliments despite the heavy showers. A complete absence of pools of water which would have been seen on a traditional type of cinder track provided immediate evidence of all that has been claimed about its unique surface.

"Honour of being the first winner at the centre went to English Schools champion Alan Pascoe (South), Britain's joint number one last season, in the 120 yards hurdles, when he clocked 14.6 seconds. It was late in the afternoon after having notched the first leg (100 yards) of the only double at the meeting, when Olympic gold medallist Lynn Davis essayed his first leap into the long jump pit.

"Taking a 19 stride run up, the 24-year-old Welshman did a jump of over a foot better than anything seen in Leicester with 24ft. 5¾ ins. Davies, 6ft. 1in. tall, set himself for his second effort and hit the sand at 25-1. Only three UK athletes have exceeded 25ft. and with Davies warming to his task anything is possible. The big one came on his third trial, 25ft. 9¾ ins., only eight inches less than his winning performance in Tokyo. 'This is a fabulous track - when can I come again?' " said the delighted Davies.

John Whetton, who won the European 1500m in his prime and later organised the Nottingham Robin Hood marathon, won the mile in 4-8.6. The fastest half mile in the country that year came from John Boulter (Achilles) in 1-50.4 and Birstall international, Jim Barry (Birchfield) won the 220 yards in 22.2. The invitation two miles walk was wildly applauded as Leicester's Geoff Toone battled to a victory in 13-34.4 from the first Commonwealth Games champion, Ron Wallwork (Lancashire).

Among local event winners were sprinters Bob Turner, a long serving highly respected Leicester Coritanians coach, John Elsley (Leicester University), Shirley Clelland (Loughborough AC) and Jean O'Neill of Lutterworth. Police multi-titled winner David Lem won the mile in 4-14.

EN-TOUT-CAS

The "K" type track at Saffron Lane was developed by the En-tout-cas company of Syston near Leicester, in co-operation with Loughborough University. Only the second of its kind in the UK - the first was at Queens University, Belfast - it was frost resistant, and had wonderful draining properties: a bucket of water emptied on it disappeared almost in seconds. Only short spikes were needed on its rubber surface.

Olympic Games have been held, and world records broken, on cinder tracks produced by the company. Ashes from a tip, collected from dustbins and deposited a century ago provided the raw materials for specialised treatment which produced superb tracks. On

Saffron Lane Sports Centre (Leicester City Council)

such surfaces, Emil Zatopek in the 10,000m at the 1948 Olympics at Wembley, and London marathon founder Chris Brasher (Melbourne 1956) won gold medals and enduring fame.

The post war Olympic Games in London in 1948 were commonly known as the "austerity Olympics". No money was available for new venues and existing grounds had to be brought up to the required standard, often within a very short space of time. En-tout-cas was engaged to lay the running track at the Empire Stadium, Wembley and the result was generally acknowledged to be a "great triumph" for the company.

In a letter to its managing director Mr C.A. Brown, Sir Arthur J. Elvin, chairman of Wembley Stadium Ltd. wrote that:

"The very fast times recorded on the Track before the weather broke, and the manner in which the track absorbed the heavy rain during the latter half of the Athletics Events, was first class evidence that the track you provided was second to none.

"The extremely favourable comments made by foreign experts, by all sections of the Press, and by the Competitors themselves, on the excellence of your Track, must have been a source of great satisfaction to you. Whilst I never had any doubt that you would be able to carry out your contract to provide a good Track in the time available, I must say the final result exceeded my expectations".

An En-tout-cas 440 yards track was laid at the Leicester University ground at Manor Road, Oadby. It survives to this day, owing much of its longevity to head groundsman for 43 years, Sidney Cadle, a recipient of the Queen's Silver Jubilee Medal. Loughborough University also has an En-tout-cas arena. Numerous world stars have performed at the Ashby Road ground, especially at the annual meeting, between Loughborough Past and Present Students, and the might of the AAA and British Students. First held in 1959, it enjoys national eminence, and regularly includes invitations to county athletes.

MEXICAN FIESTA SAFFRON LANE

The Mexicans, who became one of the most powerful of race walking nations, made the first of several visits to Leicester on December 6, 1967, early in their rise to eminence.

Initial winner Sgt. Jose Pedraza, an Olympic medallist in his own country the following year, clocked 44-5.4 for 10k, ripping 2-24.4 off the standing Mexican record. Geoff Toone (LWC) fifth, lowered the county best from 47-33 to 46-42.2.

On the second visit in 1969, Toone won in a new track record time of 43-51.8, followed by P. Colin whose 44-01 was a new Mexican record from J. Olivers 44-02 and P. Ramirez 44-36. Raul Gonzales led the November 1973 charge with yet another Mexican record of 42-37. Toone finished third in 44-18.

GREAT 10 MILE RACES AT SAFFRON LANE

Saffron Lane has played host to many memorable races and meetings, among them the AAA 10 mile championships, held there for five successive years, between 1968 and 1972.

The results were:-

1968	Ron Hill (Bolton)	47-02.2
	Ron Grove (LCAT)	48-21.8
	Wally Bent (LCAT)	49-08
1970	Trevor Wright (W/B)	47-20.2
	Ron Hill	47-35.2
	Ron Grove	47-42.2
1972	Bernard Plain (Cardiff)	48-25.8
	Tony Birks (Staffs)	48-26.4
	Keith Angus	48-35.2
1969	Ron Hill	47-27
	Ron Grove	47-28.2
	John Caine (LCAT)	48-50
1971	Trevor Wright	46-51.6
	Ron Grove	48-05.8
	Keith Angus (Sheff)	48-24.8

The first world sub 47 minutes for 10 miles on the track was run at Saffron Lane, on November 9 1968. In an event specially arranged by long distance Morpeth star Jim Alder, Ron Hill of Bolton clocked a world record of 46 minutes 44 seconds. Ron Grove, of the Leicester Colleges of Art and Technology AC (LCAT), was runner up in a county record of 47-02, and Jim Alder, third, finished in 47-29.

There were only a couple of dozen people present. There were no prizes, no free meals, no sponsorship. Grove had taken time off from work and returned to his place of employment after the race, while Ron Hill motored back north and celebrated with a fish and chip supper.

All of them competed "for the love of running."

INTER COUNTIES CHAMPIONSHIPS AT LEICESTER, 1970, 1971, 1972, 1977, 1983

After a lapse of 35 years the Inter Counties championships returned to Leicestershire, and on five occasions were staged at Saffron Lane, heralding a more glamourous phase in local athletics. The stadium with its much acclaimed track and modern facilities was much in favour, and enjoyed an edge which was unfortunately not maintained in later years, with the big time events draining away.

Prior to moving to Leicester, the last venue for the meeting in London was the White City stadium in 1969, before a crowd of 7,500. The Leicester audience was 4,500, but considered to be a satisfactory start in the provinces. There was no permanent seating in Saffron Lane at that time, so there was an expensive item to be met each time for the transportation of seating.

In the 1970 3000 metres walk, Olly Caviglioli (Essex), second, set a French national record of 12-27.4, a fine performance in keeping with his status of winning English Schools titles. His father, who accompanied him constantly, was lucky to be around. During the troubles in Algeria, he had been sentenced to death by a firing squad, but fortunately the sentence was not carried out.

Martin Higdon (Middlesex) pole vaulted 4.61m, an AAA national record. In the absence of Geoff Capes, Jeff Teale (Yorks) won the shot with 18.05m, and Leicestershire's Bill Tancred mounted the podium with a discus victory of 51.98m. A smart mile win in 4-4.2 by John Whetton was swallowed the following year, when Walter Wilkinson equalled the championship best performance with a still standing ground record of 3-56.6.

Wilkinson's splits were:- 61, 2-1.7, 3-00.6 and a 56.6 final circuit, edged out Peter Stewart 3-57.4, Brendan Foster 3-58.5, Norman Morrison 3-58.7 and disappointed Royal Marine Jim Douglas (Devon), one tenth of a second outside four minutes. There was a memorable 5000 metres, as David Black (Staffs) set his own cracking pace and a European junior record of 13-46.2. Dave Lem ran it for the county, eighth in 14-00.8. Over 10,000 metres, Mike Freary (Lancs) set a CBP of 28-52 and seventh placed John Offord clocked 29-30.4. In the long jump Alan Lerwill had spectators out of their seats with a distance of 8.12m (26ft. 7 3/4ins.). En-route to 11 successive top spots, Geoff Capes registered a shade over 60 feet with the shot, 18.29m.

In 1972, Lerwill again captured headlines, pushing the long jump distance to 8.15m

(26' 9") on a cold, windy afternoon. Paul Nihill (Surrey) completed a walking double, winning the 10,000m by three minutes in 42-34.6, a UK time only beaten by Phil Embleton, 41-55.6. The 3000m steeplechase for the En-tout-cas cup went to Steve Hollings (Yorks) in 8-39 and the 400m hurdles was won by John Sherwood (Yorks) in 52 secs, an event previously (1968) won by John Cooper, Olympic silver medallist in 51.5 when it was over 440 yards. Capes shot win was with 19.21.

On the return to the stadium in 1977 standards had dropped in some events. David Black's 5000m came in 14-7.4, Richard Milne won the 10,000 for East Midlands in 30-11.6 and Ken Cocks (Cornwall) winning long jump was with 7.30m. A good triple jump resulted in a win for David Johnson (Yorks) with 16.18m, an event won three years previously by Peter Blackburn (Coritanians) with 15.62m. County teacher Jim Whitehead (Birchfield) won the hammer (62.70) and Roger Mills (Essex) took the 3000m walk in 12-14.6. Leicester's Brian Adams, who won several titles, was number one in the 10,000m in 43-57.2.

Geoff Toone (LWC), Midland 10 mile walk champion, pictured at the County championships at Saffron Lane in June 1971. (George Herringshaw)

The 1983 meeting was a one day affair, the CAU chairman being John Smith, former county president, who had most generously and ably supported local athletics. Popular Ernie Obeng of Loughborough fame won the 100m in 10.5 (legal) and with an against wind of 2.5m, Luke (Buster) Watson blasted 20.9 for the 200m. The 400m top points went to Roy Dickens (Surrey) in 47.3, compared with a Leicestershire winner over 440 yards in 1965, the 47.2 of

Malcolm Yardley which was then a championship best performance (CBP). Dick Callan roused local enthusiasm in the 5000m as he beat Mike Chorlton (Yorks) by a tenth of a second in 13-55.6. Jeff Gutteridge with a CBP in the pole vault cleared 5.20m and in the shot it was Mike Winch running up a series, his best of three years being 18.25m. The javelin was hoisted on to a new CBP plane too by Roald Bradstock, spearing the ground at 85.26m.

Of course on other occasions outside Leicester, local athletes had a measure of success in Inter-Counties championships. World student silver medallist and 200m cup winner (Europe) Chris Monk completed the sprint double in 1973 and 1975, his fastest being 10.5 and exactly 21 secs. Dick Callan's hopes of becoming Leicester's first sub four minute miler were raised and dashed as he won in 1981 in 4-00.24.

DAIRYGATE ATHLETICS MEETINGS AT SAFFRON LANE

In 1976 the Saffron Lane track was re-surfaced, and an extra lane was added for sprints. Major events, which had fallen off in recent years, once again returned to the Stadium. Three Dairygate Athletics meetings at the start of the 80's brought to the city a galaxy of world famous stars, fortuitously before the sport turned professional.

Hundreds of thousands of pounds would be needed today to mastermind the complex operation, financed by Leicestershire Co-operative Dairies Division. It was brought about by the vision and enthusiasm of the manager Tony Morley. Money alone could not have assembled the star cast. An expert in the international field was needed to initiate the invitations, and the ideal supremo for this task was Loughborough University chief coach George Gandy, at that time working on a conditioning programme with student Sebastian Coe. Gandy persuaded an elite line-up to compete in Leicester, and gilded the occasions with superb informative commentaries in the stadium.

At the first meeting on September 7 1980, Coe had to withdraw after fighting a losing battle to get fit. Reluctantly he had to call off, but promised to come back next year as he addressed the crowd over the PA. In Coe's absence, the spotlight fell on the budding Steve Cram and Dave Moorcroft who were themselves to become world record holders. However, in a pulsating finish to the one mile, the Run the World Sports Aid torch bearer, Charnwood's Omar Khalifa of the Sudan, grabbed the honours in 4-00.3.

Cram hit the line in 4-00.7, Nick Rose who was to win an English cross country title in Leicester clocked 4-01.3, and the American Craig Masback followed in 4-01.4. Tim

Hutchings led the next finishers in 4-01.9, Moorcroft was seventh, Coritanians Dick Callan 9th, just beating in another world record holder, the mighty Kenyan, Henry Rono. European 400 metres winner David Jenkins won the 200 in 21.5 from Coritanian Derek Butler, who himself had earlier pipped clubmate Chris Monk in the 100m.

The women's mile was controlled by Christina Boxer (Aldershot) whose 4-35.2 was a ground record and removed the 4-36.8, set by Maria Gomers (Netherlands) in June 1969, which was then a world record. A brilliant 400m in 51.6 secs. from Michelle Probert, the only Welsh female to have won an Olympic medal, was at the expense of the superb young Scot, Linsey Macdonald.

A one mile walk dramatised the heel and toe business for 6-14.8, Alan King providing an excellent example of safe, fast progression, as he beat Olympian clubmate Phil Vesty. Greatest performance of the day was a new All Comers hammer throwing record, by the World record holder himself, Karl-Hans Riehm of Germany. His series consisted of:- 73.30m (240' 5"); 77.02m (252' 8"); 76.32m (250' 4"); No throw; No throw; 76.64m (251' 5").

Twelve months later, with the meeting being staged in July, another bumper crowd saluted the satin smooth running of Seb Coe, acknowledging too his honouring of that year-old pledge - 'I'll run next year.' In the midst of a glut of superb performances, Coe came up with another great run, clocking 2 mins. 17.6 secs. when winning the 1000 metres feature event from Sydney Maree, Steve Cram and Omar Khalifa. Cram finished second in 2-18.5, Maree 2-19.5, Khalifa 2-20 and in fifth Chris McGeorge, now teaching at Burleigh College, Loughborough, the 1985, World Students 1500m gold medallist. He is now Leicestershire Schools AA Secretary.

Before this grand finale the meeting had been treated to some of the best athletics seen at the stadium since it was opened in 1967. High on the list was the perfectly timed, last gasp finish of the Commonwealth Games 1500m champion, Dave Moorcroft, victor in the 3000 metres in 8-4.4. Moorcroft taught at Roundhill College, Thurmaston, and helped in the running of schools cross country leagues.

Incredibly, Moorcroft lost a shoe in an early melee, stopped, put it on, sprinted to catch the group and rejoined the action. Harborough's Dick Callan, with less than 200m to go, had fought off the attentions of Mike McLeod, the Los Angeles 10,000m Olympic silver medallist, and Tim Hutchings. A crescendo of applause for the local man was premature, as Moorcroft with a split second timed run zipped through to take Callan before the line, by a couple of metres, in 8-4.4.

American ace Emmit King grabbed the 100m in 10.5, David Jenkins, resident in Leicester, snatched the 300m in 32.9, a notable fifth spot going to the double Olympic

Decathlon gold medallist, Daley Thompson. The USA again rose to the heights in the high jump as Milton Goode soared over 2.19m (7ft. 2 1/4ins.), defeating the British top man Mark Naylor (2.16m) and compatriot Jeff Woodward, the American record holder, having an off night at 2.10m (6ft. 10 1/2ins.). Peter Yates heaved the javelin 78.28m (256ft. 9ins), and the best women's event, the 300m was won by Joslyn Hoyte-Smith who in 37.2 secs. got a photo finish verdict over Michelle Scutt, formerly Probert.

In a fine programme of club events, Katrina Butters, subsequently Mrs Kemp, set a Coritanian 800m record of 2 mins. 10 secs. A ground record came from high jumper Diana Elliott, the Leicester girl clearing 1.87m (6ft. 1 1/2ins.). Glenys Morton long jumped 6.33m (20ft. 9 1/4 ins.), beating Coritanian clubmate Diana Elliott, second with 5.95m (19ft. 6 1/4ins.). In the curtain falling year of 1982, the Olympic 100 metres champion Alan Wells provided an impressive display of sprinting. He completed a double in 10.7

Dick Callan (LC), Inter Counties mile champion and 5k international,competing here for the AAA at Loughborough in June 1980. (George Herringshaw)

secs. and 20.9, but felt that he still had a lot of work to do if he was to win a European gold medal in Athens in September. Wells told the *Leicester Mercury*'s Peter Grundy: "It was my first competition of the season and I was just too psyched up. My mental attitude is so important and it's not right yet. But I will put things right."

In damp and dismal conditions, the New Zealander John Walker, the 1976 Olympic 1500 metres champion and the first man to run a mile in under 3-50, was a convincing 1000 metres winner in 2-21.3. "I was happy with my performance," said the New Zealander who planned to move up to 5,000 metres like Seb Coe for the 1984 Olympics. While not the force of six or seven years ago, Walker was still a fabulous performer and destroyed a talented field of internationals. Walker, courteous, charming and informative about his approach to training, was most appreciative that he had been invited to run in Leicester.

So ended one of the most fascinating periods in local athletics, immense thanks being due to the Co-op Dairies Division Marketing Manager, Tony Morley.

SPECIAL OLYMPICS, 20-25 AUGUST 1989

The Special Olympics originated in the United States, but the movement covers over 70 nations all over the world, enabling people with learning disabilities to take part in a wide range of sporting activities. The first Special Olympic games to be held in Britain took place on Merseyside in 1982, and the second in Brighton in 1986. With around 2500 participants from the UK, and visiting teams from France and Germany, the third Games in 1989 were the largest sporting event ever to be held in Leicester. In the words of Derek Fryett, Chairman of the Special Olympics Games Council, "When Leicester heard it had been successful in its bid to stage the 1989 UK Special Olympics, we realised we had embarked on one of the biggest projects in the city's history".

Immediately a marshalling of resources was put in place. Raising huge sums of money and bedding down a base organisation was dependent on the co-operation of Leicester City Council, Leicestershire County Council, local district councils, community groups, and over 4000 volunteers from all walks of life. The Games also received major support from the University of Leicester, the Chamber of Commerce, the British Shoe Corporation, the Lions Club, and other local sponsors.

On 19 August 1989, a service in Leicester Cathedral was followed by a wonderful march past in opening ceremony on the Tigers' pitch on Welford Road. The Olympic flag was raised, and competitor Sylvia Motley lit the Olympic flame with the torch brought from Brighton by Leicestershire Prison Officers, running relays over the 155 miles and stopping at prisons en route overnight. The emotional oath of the Special Olympics was proclaimed: "LET ME WIN, BUT IF I CANNOT WIN, LET ME BE BRAVE IN THE ATTEMPT".

A wide range of facilities was allocated for the various events, with cycling and athletics held at Saffron Lane Sports Centre. Athletes with joy on their faces, some in wheelchairs, some struggling for leg movement, captured constant attention. The stream of medal presentations for running and allied events was announced by Sarah Sharlott and the brothers Phil and Brian Owen. Sporting stars dropped in at various venues to lend their support, among them super soccer stars Gary Lineker and Gordon Banks, and Games President Sir Eldon Griffiths MP congratulated Leicester on a job well done.

Responsibility for steering the various activities rested on the Special Olympics organising team led by Granby Halls Manager and Games Director Terry Harrison. "When this moment is over", he wrote in the Games Souvenir Brochure, "the best memories will be of the friends you have met and the hearts that you have touched"; but as he said of the competitors at the closing ceremony, "in helping them, we too have become winners".

Following the Games, the East Midlands Initiative Trust was formed in 1990 to give continuing support to sporting activities for people with learning disabilities.

8 CLUB SCENE

A roll call of local clubs since the 1860s would be a lengthy one. Some have been shortlived, others have enjoyed a long and illustrious history, and the road running boom of recent years has added to the list. Several of these clubs, like the Leicester Harriers, the Leicester Walking Club, and Leicester University, are highlighted elsewhere. Foremost among others worthy of attention are Leicester Colleges of Art and Technology.

LEICESTER COLLEGES OF ART AND TECHNOLOGY AC (LCAT)

Blackbird Road playing fields were home to the club, which came to prominence with the annual inter-departmental sports from the 1930s.

Pharmacy were outstanding. Among their talented athletes were Margaret Parker, Midland 100m champion, who emigrated to Australia, and county cross country number one, Reg Rowlands. Head of Pharmacy was Mr Colin Gunn, a long time president of the athletic club, whose office hosted committee meetings. County track and field championships were staged from there, and Midlands and inter-counties cross country. In an Art and Tech v Loughborough Students match, European sprint champion Jack Archer, international Ken Jones, and the club's international Ron Toone met in a hectic 100 yards. Archer won his heat in 9.9 seconds, but Ken Jones won the final in 9.7. The Colleges of Art and Technology were of course the forerunners of Leicester Polytechnic, now DeMontfort University.

BUSINESS HOUSE CLUBS

By the 1920s, a growing number of local companies were providing sports facilities for their employees as part of industrial welfare schemes. One was the Wolsey company, international hosiery manufacturers, whose annual sports often featured visiting star athletes, and whose Aylestone ground was said to be "the finest sports ground in Leicester". It was here in 1928 that the American Harold Osborn, high jump and decathlon champion at the 1924 Paris Olympics, became the first man to clear six feet in the high jump in Leicester.

On Saturday, August 18 1928, at the Wolsey Sports Ground in Aylestone, Osborn the world record holder gave a "fine exhibition jump, clearing six feet one inch, with comparative ease, combining grace with his effort", the *Leicester Evening Mail* reported. Photographs show his dropping down to the ground - no air filled beds in those days - with what in some reports is described as a side clearance. Actually he was the best exponent of the Western Roll, the technique of turning the body over the bar, in his time.

Winner of an AAA title too, Osborn was noted for a legal if questionable skill. Going over the bar, he could force it back with his hand against the upright and supporting peg, a little insurance against it falling off. He may have tried this trick at Glasgow Rangers Sports on August 1 1925, when he leaped 6 feet 6³/₈ inches. It was not ratified as a British record, but it led to Olympic gold medallist, Harold Abrahams, being asked to draft a rule making it obligatory for the cross bar to be able to fall off in either direction. The flat pegs were one and a half inches wide.

There was no criticism of his method at Leicester and his performance was widely acclaimed. But how did Osborn become available to jump in Leicester? It was due to the initiative of the manager of Wolsey Sports and Welfare Club, Mr Edward Lowe, responsible for organising the annual sports. Mr Lowe, had been over to Amsterdam for the 1928 Olympic Games, and arranged for several of the American team to come to the city, along with Jose Barrientos, the Cuban 100/200 metres champion. The *Leicester Evening Mail* (now defunct) and the *Leicester Mercury* previewed the sports as the greatest ever held in the Midlands.

One advertisement proclaimed:

**WHAT EVER HAPPENS -
DON'T MISS THE WOLSEY SPORTS
ON SATURDAY
NEVER BEFORE IN LEICESTER
HAS SUCH A STUPENDOUS SPORTS
PROGRAMME BEEN ARRANGED
ONE CONTINUOUS ROUND OF
THRILLS AND EXCITEMENT
WORLD FAMOUS ATHLETES
COMPETING
ADMISSION 1s 2d (One shilling and
two pence) including tax
Children under 14s 6d (2.5 pence)
GRANDSTANDS EXTRA**

Osborn's effort was the highlight, but a "very interesting innovation was the use of Loud Speakers for the purpose of announcing results. Sixteen loud speakers joined in pairs,

*Chris Monk (LC), European Cup 200m champion and AAA champion, winning the County Schools 100m championship at Leicester in June 1970.
(George Herringshaw)*

were spread around the ground at frequent intervals and in addition, two more in the horticultural tent." They were of exactly the same type used at Stamford Bridge and "this is the FIRST OCCASION ON WHICH SUCH A METHOD OF ANNOUNCING RESULTS HAS BEEN USED ON ANY LEICESTER SPORTS GROUND."

As a footnote to Osborn's jump, David Rodgers was the first athlete to get over six feet in a Leicestershire championship, with a clearance of 6ft. 0½in. in 1952 in the junior event at Saffron Lane from a grass take off. In 1965 his Art and Tech. clubmate, Colin Brand, from cinders at Manor Road, achieved 6ft. 1 in. in the senior test. Subsequently, two Leicester Coritanian ladies, WAAA champions, Brenda Gibbs and Diana Davies, both cleared six feet.

The British United Shoe Machinery Company of Belgrave - commonly known as the BU - also had its own sports ground at Mowmacre Hill. For many years the annual sports were a regular feature, with BU athletes training there several times a week in preparation for these and other events. George White (also of LCAT) arranged coaching, and athletic and social club secretary Geoff Hasnip, an AAA treasurer, organised the sports. A Groocock Trophy meeting, named for one of the directors, involved many leading clubs.

The appearance here of the 1948

Dave Lem Snr. (LC and Police), international athlete , winner of two Midland senior cross country titles, and of numerous Police championships. Pictured at Crystal Palace in 1974. (George Herringshaw)

Olympic 400 metres champion Arthur Wint (Jamaica), and E.A. McDonald Bailey of Trinidad and London Polytechnic, winner of 14 AAA 100 and 220 yards titles, made 1947 the best remembered of the BU sports. In a short limit 100 yards invitation handicap Mac had been asked to take on the best of the City athletes. They included BU's Bernard Bindley, international Ron Toone, Fred Clay, Brian Kirk, M.E.F. Gray, Dick Collett and G. Wilson.

Mac, off scratch, "with quick mincing strides, an American idea," said the *Leicester Mercury*, won with a yard or so to spare, and a crowd of about 5000 gave him an ecstatic reception". And then came Wint, whose appearance was unscheduled. Wint, who qualified as a doctor, and in more recent years was a High Commissioner for Jamaica in London, had come with Mac to see his brother, who was serving at an RAF station in Leicestershire. BU secretary Geoff Hasnip placed a car at Wint's disposal, a pleasant reunion followed, and to show his appreciation, Arthur readily consented to run in a quickly arranged race over 400 metres. Wint's enormous near nine feet stride captivated everybody's attention and gave him an easy victory. It was a superb occasion, so that years afterwards "I was there" was a very proud claim.

FASTEST MP FOR WEST LEICESTER
Greville Janner, MP for West Leicester, in his student days beat 14 times AAA sprint champion, E. A. McDonald Bailey, in a handicap at Motspur Park, London.

Another dimension of works athletics was expressed with regular relay meetings. Trophies included the English Electric Cup for a 4 x 110 yards relay; the Petfoods Cup for a one mile team race; and the City of Leicester Cup for a one mile medley relay (880, 220, 220 and 440 yards).

Interest was at its greatest between 1935 and 1968, and several well-known local companies were among the winners. They included the BU, Jones and Shipman, Mellor Bromley, the Co-op Wheatsheaf works, English Electric, Petfoods of Melton Mowbray, Brush of Loughborough, and the National Gas Turbine Establishment (NGTE) at Whetstone.

BELGRAVE UNITED AC

From the early 1950s the Belgrave club was based at the Police recreation ground on Melton Road, at the invitation of the Chief Constable Mr O.J.B. Cole.

Enthusiasm pushed aside the drawback of it hardly being a suitable field on which to produce top class athletes. Wooden dressing rooms packed to capacity sufficed, and the club survived with Olympians Pat Lowe, John Cooper and Malcolm Yardley starting their careers here. Cross country runners of the medal winning calibre of Mick Oakland,

Bill Baker, Dave Parker and Don Nadin, managed their speed work from it. The sudden death of the president in the 1960s ended the Police connection, for the athletes were turned away on the appointment of a new chief. Belgrave were given a temporary home at Corah's ground on Thurcaston Road, and later amalgamated with Art and Tech.

LEICESTER CORITANIANS

Almost 2 years after the opening of the Saffron Lane Sports Centre, on April 1 1969, the majority of county clubs amalgamated to form the Leicester Coritanians, a monopoly of immense potential. The natural city successors to Leicester Harriers and Art and Tech, Coritanians have risen to many heights in team and individual events. They have a superb record in women's cross country championships, listed separately, and a string of internationals and winners in national and area meetings.

Top in sentimental memory is the late Dave Lem Snr. who was known nationwide in police circles for his road, track and cross achievements, and was a household name throughout the county, stemming from his early appearances in athletics when at New Parks School, Leicester. Dave was highly respected as a community policeman, and was over the moon when his son David followed in his footsteps by winning the County senior cross country title.

Craig Mochrie (LC), first Leicester born man to run a sub-four minute mile. Midland 5000m CBP, and winner of Inter Counties cross country title. (George Herringshaw)

Dick Callan, an international indoors and out, held centre stage creating some times that have only been beaten recently. On the formation of a club in his home town of Market Harborough, he naturally gravitated to them and helped with coaching. John

Denham won the AAA youths steeplechase championship and was a member of the county junior cross team that fairly recently won bronze medals at Corby in the inter counties. Phil Makepeace made the team for the international Cross Country. Joey Masterson and Andrew Hart have won numerous road races, especially in the city and county, and Matthew Barker with a sub 1-49 over 800m, is at an early stage of his career.

The last three or four years have in many ways been quite tremendous as national titles were amassed by Carl Southam (later to join Charnwood). Helen Frost, Helen Titterington, Maxine Newman, Lisa York and Andrew Lynch, who cleared 2.16m in the high jump. British students champions, Elliott and Jason Dronfield have both won high jump titles. The achievements of many other Coritanians are acknowledged elsewhere, but one or two deserve a special mention here.

Craig Mochrie, an inspirational athlete, gave notice of a career to come with an English Schools victory. A graduate of Loughborough Technical College and Loughborough College of Art, he twice ran with distinction in the World Cross Country Championships, earning a team silver in 1989.

Also in 1989 he came fourth in the Commonwealth Games Trial Race at 5000 metres, before going on to record his best ever time of 13-26.74 in the Van Damme Memorial Meeting in Brussels. In the same year, he became the first Leicester man to run a sub-four minute mile, at Berry Hill, Mansfield, in 3-59.6, and in 1993, recaptured his cross country crown at the Parklands, Wigston.

At Meadowbank Stadium, Edinburgh in 1973 spectators erupted in admiration, and millions watching on TV exulted at the superb drive of Chris Monk, as he won the European Cup 200m final at the age of 21. Etched in the memory is his technical brilliance rounding the top bend, and escaping from the cream of the continent. Against a head wind of 3.3 metres per second, Britain's first ever winner of the race clocked a remarkable 21 secs - sheer brilliance under the adverse conditions - as East Germany's Hans-Jurgen Bombach finished in 21.05 and Ossie Karttunen (Finland) in 21.24.

That was the peak moment of his career, influenced by AAA senior coach John Bailey who had come to the city from the north. Monk, a Moat schoolteacher and Leicester Coritanian, had three weeks earlier in August, in Moscow, run a magnificent career best of 20.7 secs, for a second spot in the World Student Games.

Italy's Pietro Mennea, a later breaker of the world record, shaded Monk in 20.7. In the same 1973 season, Monk achieved the ambition of all sprinters in winning an AAA title (21.1). An American, Mark Lutz succeeded to the title 12 months later. Lutz had run fourth to Monk in the Students Games in Moscow.

In January 1974, in Christchurch, New Zealand, Chris (21.3) ran sixth for England. The world record breaker Don Quarrie (Jamaica) won in 20.7 and in seventh, David Jenkins of Scotland in 21.5. Indoors and outdoors, Monk won many titles and enjoyed international occasions across the world. He retired entitled to be classed as the city's greatest sprinter. Among the other greats who could be singled out are George Brewill, a turn of the century man, first local winner of the AAA 200yds crown and Roland Toone of Rothley (Art and Tech).

The 1974 Midland Boys 800m Championship saw one of the club's outstanding team performances.

The first five to finish in an entry of 22, were all Leicester Coritanians. Results:-

1 Robert Slater 2-6; 2 Roy Wilson 2-7.5; 3 Wayne Walker 2-8.3; 4 Gary Burdett 2-8.8; 5 Steve Long 2-9.2.

Leicester Coritanians women's teams competed in the 1975 Motorway League and then the National League in 1977. In 1992 they were elected to membership of the Daily Telegraph UK Women's Athletics League's newly formed fifth division, winning the first match at Saffron Lane Stadium with 272 points from Thurrock (262½) and Radley (260).

Coritanians have had many dedicated coaches. Irrespective of whether they are highly qualified or have feet on varying rungs of the ladder, their contributions have been invaluable. They include John Bailey (Chris Monk), Paul Blissett (Matthew Barker), John Price (Helen Titterington), Malcolm Smith (Diana Davies), Ellie Binks (Andrew Lynch), Roger Binks (Robbie Singh), Merv Wilson (Arif Shah), Jenny Burtonwood (MD squad), June Clarke (javelin), Tony Clarke (sprints), Pete Barber (Claire Howard), Sandra and Tony Salmon (young athletes) and David Couling (decathlon).

Currently, Bill Burdett is guiding a stream of hurdlers who include 1993 English School No. 1, Louise Colledge, Deanne Kenney, Midland winner and Schools international, and English Schools silver medallist Pete Donovan. In the young athletes leagues, Midlands and Heart of England, managed by Shirley Dronfield, Coritanians built an impressive launch pad for 1994. They will be competing in the Premier sections and will be joined by local rivals Charnwood and Oadby and Wigston Legionnaires.

Leicester Coritanians take their name from the Latin word Coritani, used to describe the British tribe settled in this area at the time of the Roman conquest of England in the first century AD. In more recent years, however, archaeologists have re-interpreted the evidence, and concluded that the tribe should be properly known as the Corieltauvi.

CHARNWOOD AC

No account of local clubs would be complete without a mention of Charnwood Athletic Club. Formed 18 years ago and with a current membership of over 400, Charnwood has produced a stream of athletes who have excelled on road, track and cross country. Based at Loughborough University, they train on an all weather track.

Their January cross country relays, currently from Hind Leys School, Shepshed, are sometimes contested by more than 100 men's teams. Launched in 1978 on the University campus, building developments influenced a move to Shepshed. In the past three years George Gandy's keen students from the University have beaten all comers, but they have some way to go to catch up on Charnwood who reeled off six in the 1980's. Fastest lap heroes from Charnwood include Andy Armitage, Jack Buckner, Adrian Royle and Dave Driver.

In the women's relays, covering half the distance of the men's, Charnwood and Coritanians have vied for honours, the latter leading 3 to 2. At Shepshed however, it has been Derby all the way. The Charnwood half marathon was an enormous success from its inaugural. Like several other road events numbers declined, but on August 1 1993 a Running Riot programme was put on with one mile, 5km and 10km events, which went well.

Jack Buckner's superb European 5km victory at Stuttgart in 1986 (13-10.15), his two Olympic appearances and running in Commonwealth and Worlds are highlighted in the "Olympians". The brilliant marathon running of county record holder Jackie Davies (2-38-22) in Berlin and the half marathon local best of Rosemary Duddle (73-35) and the 10 miles (55-19), reflect the many talents of Charnwood.

In young athletes leagues, Charnwood can look forward to a great 1994 season. Six golds in the Midland championships is a statement of their ability. Mark Edwards a number one national junior shot putter, set a perfect example with two golds for he also won the discus. Matthew Pilkington (javelin), Jenna Allen (javelin), David Butler (long jump) and Lisa Worden (800) rounded off with a club record in the under 15, with 2-18.1.

Charnwood's coaching enthusiasts include marathon man Roy Stowell (a diet expert), Martin Goosey, Ivan Taylor, Lionel Lambourne, Peter Clarke, Stuart Walker, Ben Boldy, Jim Edwards. Co-ordinator is Peter Rake and he is creating a pool of pole vaulters, not seen before in the county.

LEICESTERSHIRE ATHLETIC AND
ROAD RUNNING CLUBS AND EVENTS

Competitors from Leicester often compete in events held by other county clubs. This is a full list of Leicestershire clubs and events.

Barrow Runners	*The six miles, Festival 10 miles. Draws maximum Winter League fields, record 425*
Beaumont Leys RC	*Road 5k's (from Shopping Centre)*
	Five miles, old BU grounds, Mowmacre Hill
Bowline Climbing Club	*Instant classic. Anstey, via Old John, Beacon Hill (12 miles)*
Braunstone Town Runners	*Exhilarating, Mallory Park car racing circuit, 10k*
Charnwood AC	*The 13.1. Transferred to Running Riot 10k*
Coalville Harriers	*Toughest league six. Bardon Hill Challenge*
	Castle Rock School to the top and back
Dee-Lux	*Real cross country. "Mud and Muck"*
Desford Striders	*Only quarter marathon locally*
GEC Harriers, Whetstone	*10 miles, 20 miles, hosts Pace relay (including county championships)*
Harborough AC	*Gartree 5 miles*
Huncote Harriers	*Wakes 5 miles, the Eight, real cross, mud in technicolour*
Leicester Coritanians	*Superb record in women's cross championships*
	County and N. Midlands league on Western Park
Leicester Constabulary	*Proud record on National Police road, cross and track*
Leicestershire County Council	*Seven miles (league) from County Hall*
Leicester University	*Long standing hosts at Manor Road Grounds*
Loughborough University	*Excellence in athletics attainment*
Lutterworth Swifts	*Small club that contests league events*
Nuneaton Harriers	*(Affiliated to County AAA) The Atherstone 13.1. (merged with Hinckley) AC and high class veterans squad AC*
Oadby and Wigston Legionnaires	*Youth development. The Wigston 7*
Birstall Running Club (Ex-Oliver)	*The 7 miles, league race, at Countesthorpe*
Races	*Racers Anonymous Club, Earl Shilton*
Roadhoggs	*The 15k from Groby CC*
Rutland AC	*Mini marathon from Oakham. Adjacent London marathon date. Huge entry*
Shepshed AC	*Shepshed 10K (Hind Leys School)*
Stilton Striders	*13.1, new course 10 miles. Hosts Livingston relay and league events at the Mine, Asfordby*
Thurnby Harriers	*Has promoted league events. Keen and friendly members*
West End Runners	*Assisted by Leicester City Council and Police when founded*
	Dave Lem Memorial fives
Wreake Runners	*The Wolsey Hungarton 7. Real cross*
Leicester Walking Club	*Oldest county club. Mercury walk and open 7*

9 OLYMPIANS

Since the first modern Olympics in 1896, thousands of British athletes have competed in the Olympic Games, among them some notable figures with local connections.

A.R. Mills DCM

b. 16.1.1894
Leicester Harriers
Marathon
VII Olympic Games
Antwerp 1920
VIII Olympic Games
Paris 1924

Leicester Harrier Bobby Mills was a Lincolnshire farmer who lived at Eastriell, near Boston. He was made welcome at the club after being put in touch with its secretary, Freddy Cox. Mills had no known athletics background, but he was tough enough to survive four years of trench warfare in World War One, in which he was awarded the Distinguished Conduct Medal.

He set a British marathon record at his first attempt over the distance in the 1920 Polytechnic marathon, Windsor Park to Chiswick, in 2-37-40.4. The AAA marathon championship had not been introduced then, but the Polytechnic was always regarded as the unofficial national championship.

In the same year, Mills was chosen to run for England in the international cross country championship in Belfast. He finished sixth over a 10 miles course and England won the team race.

Most weekends, Mills ran from Spence Street baths to fields at Humberstone. He also ran time trials on city roads and when he went to Antwerp to run on August 22, only five weeks had elapsed between his first and second marathon.

The Times of August 23 described the race. There were 47 runners and Gitsham (South Africa) led at the first kilometre by two yards from Hans Kolehmainen (Finland). At 13 kilometres, though the leading British runner, Mills had fallen 500 yards behind. There was no further mention of him and he finished outside the top ten. The official distance was 26 miles 990 yards (42,750 metres) the longest marathon in Olympic history.

Subsequently Mills completed a hat trick in the Poly marathon, winning in 1921 and 1922. He was second in 1923 and third in 1924. He ran for England in the international cross country championship in 1921 and 1923. His greatest effort was runner-up in 1921 at Newport, only 10 seconds behind the winner, W. Freeman of Birchfield. He represented Britain again in the 1924 Paris Olympics, where the marathon distance became standardised at 26 miles 385 yards. However, he failed to finish.

Tebbs Lloyd Johnson

b. 7.4. 1900
Leicester Walking Club
50km road walk
XI Olympic Games
Berlin 1936
XIV Olympic Games
London 1948

Lloyd Johnson himself drafted an account of his 25 years in top class walking in the *Race Walking Record*, of February 1946:

"The story opens in 1920 when I was persuaded by a well known Midlands walker, F.W. Preston, to try my paces with the Leicester Harriers, who at that time had a small walking section. I decided to try myself out in a few races, so in 1921 entered in a one mile handicap in Birmingham and from the 170 yards mark was very narrowly beaten for first place. This early success was naturally such a stimulus that I entered in as many races as I conveniently could, with the result that I picked up quite a few prizes in track handicaps and also finished second in both the Midland Counties 2 miles championship and also second in the Birmingham Walking Club's "Bishop's Walk" of 20 miles. In fact in my first year I won a prize in every race in which I competed, with the exception of the R.W.A. (Race Walking Association) Senior at Chislehurst and the AAA open 7 at Stamford Bridge…

"In 1936 I started off well in this Olympic Games year by winning the Bishop's, the Leicester Mercury, the Midland Counties 20 mile championship, and although I had an off day in the RWA senior, only finishing 4th, I was again chosen to go to Paris but again didn't seem to settle down and only managed fourth. Then came the 50 kilos championship which was to be the trial for the Olympic Games selection.

"This was a wonderful race, Whitlock, Hopkins, Bentley and myself kept together for about 28 miles when I fell back somewhat, but with about 3 miles to go I tried one of my 1934 bursts and not only made up lost ground but went into the lead. Whitlock was the only one to challenge and we raced away neck and neck at a terrific pace to within a few hundred yards of the finish, when Harold put in a flash of speed that I could not quite match, but he passed the post only 4 seconds ahead, both of us inside the world's best figures for the distance.

Imagine my disappointment to be informed that I had been disqualified for an alleged infringement earlier in the race. However, the sting was taken out of this blow when I learnt that in spite of it, I had been selected as one of Great Britain's team.

"Perhaps I should have been content with that, but I felt I had to justify my inclusion as there had been some press comment and the following week, I competed in Lewis's Outer Circle Walk, where I knew Bentley and Rickards, who were the next in line for the Games were competing. Unfortunately I had to race very hard to beat Fred Rickards, only just getting the better of him in the sprint in.

"Many people thought I had made a big mistake in taking part in this race, instead of saving my energy for the Games. I don't want to dwell on the Berlin Games but the fact that Whitlock beat me only by 4 secs at Derby and by 20 minutes in Berlin is obvious proof that something was wrong." Lloyd Johnson finished well down the field, and Harold Whitlock, of course, won the 50 kilometres walk in Berlin, our only individual winner setting an Olympic record of 4 hrs. 30 mins 52 secs.

Johnson, however, became a sporting legend in the city mainly as a result of his exploits in the Leicester Mercury 20 miles road walk. He won the first four Mercury

Walks, eventually made it nine, was never out of the first three, and was idolised wherever he was recognised.

Born in 1900 and aged 48 at the time of the 1948 Olympic Games in London, it was unlikely that such a veteran could qualify for the British team, let alone take on the world. Nevertheless he made the squad.

As the official report of the Games noted: "At 35,000 metres, Whitlock was forced to retire, and Martineau began to lose ground. Ljunggren on the other hand, walking smoothly and in delightful style entered the Stadium three quarters of a mile ahead of his nearest rival. Behind him, the 48-year-old Johnson made a superlative effort to hold on to second place, but had to give way to Godel of Switzerland in the closing stages. Martineau was fifth". Ljunggren won in a time of 4 hrs. 41 mins. 52 secs., and Johnson peaked his career with an Olympic bronze medal, the oldest man in the Olympic Games to date to gain an individual award.

Ken Johnson
b.14.10.28
Leicester Colleges of Art and Technology AC
3000 metres steeplechase
XV Olympic Games
Helsinki 1952

World War II prevented the 1940 Olympics being held in Finland, so 12 years later, one of the greatest athletics nations was proud to host a magnificent occasion. Recognised as a most knowledgeable country in the track and field sphere, Finland could lay claim to many Olympic records, including the steeplechase, set at 9 mins. 3.8 secs. by V. Iso-Hollo, in Berlin in 1936. Ken Johnson came to the 1 mile 1,521 yards race via a successful cross country and one miling career at county level. After Helsinki he twice won the Midland mile crown, his best time being 4-15.4. However it was in the winter of 1951 that he switched to the four barriers and water jump test in each of seven laps. He constructed his own hurdle which he carried on his shoulder from Belgrave to

Ken Johnson (G. Herringshaw)

Rushey Fields, and practised relentlessly. The Whitsun Inter-Counties saw him make his steeplechase debut which was then over two miles. He ran 10-24.6 and in his next test broke a 19-year old Midland championship best performance in 10-28.

Now for the three A's championships. Peter Segedin (Yugoslavia) was here to complete a hat trick. In the race he held his own until half way when he was overtaken by Loughborough student, John Disley and Chris Brasher, gold medallist in the steeplechase four years later in Melbourne. Disley won in a championship best of 9-44, Brasher was second, and Johnson in only his third chase almost caught Segedin on the line. Ken ran 10-6.8 and as a third homelander expected to be in. He wasn't. In the British team of 65 athletes Brasher and Disley were named but not Johnson. There was angry reaction in athletics circles and after a campaign of protest, Ken knew he had been added to the squad when he received a letter from the Duke of Edinburgh.

In an event where the standards were rocketing, Ken finished seventh of 12 in 9-27 in heat one in the Olympic Stadium and did not qualify for the final. The Russian, V. Kazantsev won the heat in a new Olympic record time of 8-58. The final went to Horace Ashenfelter (USA) in 8-45.4, with Kazantsev taking the silver.

Johnson subsequently enjoyed a high standard international career, and was given the chance to show his paces in 1954 when the British United Shoe Machinery Co., Leicester, put on the Midland steeplechase championship on their Mowmacre Hill grounds, when it was staged over two miles for the last time. The heavy wooden barriers (five) were made by the BU and the excavated water jump was filled by the firm's own fire brigade, running a long hosepipe, supervised by Fire Chief, Stan Quick. Ken won easily in 10-12.4. He won five Midland championships in a row and probably missed a sixth in 1956 when the race wasn't held. His career peak came in 1954 when he won the AAA title in his fastest time of 9-00.8. Eventually the solid wooden hurdles took on a new lease of life. They were donated to Saffron Lane Sports Centre and used as crowd control barriers.

Donald Cobley

b. 17.10.28
Hinckley TC Royal Air Force
Modern Pentathlon
XVI Olympic Games
Melbourne 1956
XVII Olympic Games
Rome 1960

Don Cobley, one of the county's greatest all round athletes, won an Olympic event, but it did not qualify him for a gold medal. The official report, by Lt. Col. O.G.W. White, DSO, Manager of Great Britain's Modern Pentathlon team in 1956, is quoted. "For the cross country running we returned to the grounds of the Oaklands Hunt Club, where the winner was Sgt. D. Cobley of Britain in 13 mins. 35.5. secs. - a clear 13 secs. ahead of Haase of Sweden. This was the fastest time for this event in an Olympic Games and was mainly responsible for Britain gaining second place in the team reckoning." There were 40 entered and 37 ran, and for the first time Britain was not represented by Officers, but by Other Ranks.

The 1956 squad spent a lot of time training in the city. Hours of sustained practice were carried out at Cossington Street baths in Belgrave, as well as at Loughborough College. They were billeted at the Army Vetinary Corps quarters at Melton, where they carried out horse riding and shooting trials.

Cobley, a regular in the RAF and a PTI Sgt. set a steeplechase record for his service, won the County senior cross country title, three miles track and had also taken swimming honours. He won the Imperial Services Modern Pentathlon crown and besides several international appearances competed in the World event, held in Hungary.

It takes five days to stage a Modern Penthalon and often it takes several hours during the processing of the five events. It consists of a time and obstacle horse riding trial (5000m), fencing (epee), swimming 300m free style, cross country running (4000m) and revolver shooting (20 shot rapid fire in series of five at 20 metres).

Cobley's superb performance in the Melbourne cross country was only the third time a British Pentathlon man had won the event. Cobley gained two further distinctions. He proved to be the best member of the British team, scoring more points than his two compatriots. His winning time in the cross country was the fastest performance by over half a minute compared with the other two post-war Olympic races. Four years later, Don competed in Rome, when he was then in his 32nd year.

Malcolm Yardley

b. 23.12.40
Belgrave United AC;
Birchfield Harriers
400m and 1600m relay
XVII Olympic Games Rome
1960

Malcolm Yardley, quite small compared with the physique of many quarter milers, had enormous leg drive. His early training was on the grass at the Belgrave club's HQ, the Police Recreation Ground, Melton

Road, where two other Olympians, Pat Lowe and John Cooper, began their careers. He attracted attention in his school's annual sports and an interested teacher, Doug Smart, himself a County champion and winner of the Toone Shield (150 yds), sent him to Belgrave. He originally excelled as a half miler and in a Leicestershire Schools junior championship ran faster than the All-England championship best performance. He later unveiled a quarter mile career of great promise.

On the evening of June 15 1955 at the University College track, Manor Road, fourteen year old Yardley equalled the All-England junior record

Malcolm Yardley
(George Herringshaw)

(under 15), over 440 yds. Given an outside lane as a guest, he blasted 52.7 secs. which remained a county record until August 1992, when it was beaten by Oliver Bennett (51.87) of Leicester Coritanians.

Malcolm won Public Schools and All-England one lap titles, received a call-up again Russia when he was 16, and took Midland and AAA junior titles.

Yardley was the first 16 year old athlete to break 50 seconds for a quarter-mile, and he was twice listed in the Age Records of *Athletics Weekly* in 1965. As a 17 year-old he had run the fastest 48.5 for 440 yards (48.2m), and when only 13 ran the half mile in 2 mins. 6 secs. In the Olympic trial in 1960, Yardley qualified in 46.9 and a week later on August 13, at White City achieved a winning career peak of 46.6. In the humidity and heat of Rome, however, Malcolm didn't break 47 secs.

John Cooper
b.18.12.40
Belgrave United AC
Leicester CAT Birchfield Harriers
400m hurdles silver medallist ; silver medallist 4 X 400m relay (1964)
XVIII Olympic Games Tokyo 1964
XIX Olympic Games Mexico City 1968

Less than a decade had elapsed since John Cooper's great moments in the Tokyo

Olympic Games before he was killed in the Paris air disaster of 1974. Returning from an international Rugby football match where he had been on athletic shoe business, John perished when a faulty door on his plane led to it plunging to earth out of control. The sporting world mourned his departure and paused to look again closely at a quite remarkable career. The pinnacle was Tokyo in 1964 but the blossoming process to twice standing on the Olympic rostrum began locally.

As a youth he ran in the North Midlands cross country league as a member of Belgrave United AC, a city club based at the Police Recreation Ground, Melton Road. John was one of three Olympians to emanate from that most enthusiastic of clubs, spurred on by its eager founder secretary Reg Burton, and coaches like Eric Gutteridge.

In Leicestershire AAA championships, both in younger age groups and as a senior he had won titles in 100, 220, 440 and 880 yards. In his eventual speciality he had triumphed in 220 and 440 yards hurdles and had won high and long jumps. He could run a 1 min 52.6 secs half mile, and to further add to his versatility profile he won the English Schools intermediate triple jump in 1957. Very quick to learn, John had obvious decathlon potential, but his great energy and dedication moved in the direction of the

John Cooper (E. D. Lacey)

one lap hurdles. He went to Loughborough College and was moulded very quickly by coach Geoff Gowan in 1961. His annual best marks for the 440 yards hurdles were: 1960, 56.5; 1961, 52.3; 1962, 52.2; 1963, 50.8. He qualified for the British Olympic team with a win in the AAA championship in 51.1.

The annual fixture, Loughborough past and present students v the Amateur Athletic Association, provided opportunities to see John Cooper in action. Between 1964 and 1968, John won the one lap hurdles three times. His first pair of 52.1 set and then equalled the meeting record and his last success came in 51.7.

In the words of Melvyn Watman, in his obituary piece, in *Athletics Weekly* of March 16 1974:

"John Cooper was one of the most tenacious competitors I have ever seen and an inspiration to all around him; a man who by hard work, perseverance and grit rose to the heights of Olympic silver medallist......In the context of 400m hurdling history he was Britain's finest competitor since the days of Lord Burghley in the late 1920's and early 1930's, and the immediate predecessor of David Hemery, John Sherwood and Alan Pascoe."

Of John's performance in Tokyo: "The powerfully built Birchfield Harrier went to Tokyo ranked tenth for the year among the contenders with 50.6, equalled the UK record with 50.5 in his heat, improved to 50.4 in the semi-finals and was placed second to the American favourite Rex Cawley in the final with 50.1.

John was riding on the crest of a wave; and after a 45.8 relay leg in the heats he contributed a 45.6 stage in the final to gain, along with Tim Graham, Adrian Metcalfe and Robbie Brightwell, another silver medal, the team running a superb European record of 3-01.6 behind the USA.

"Those races in Tokyo constituted the peak of John's career. The sparkle was missing in 1965 and he was injured in 1966 but he made a good comeback in 1968, to reach the Olympic semi finals in Mexico City and clock 50.8, his best time since Tokyo.

"John Cooper will be remembered with admiration and affection by all of us who were privileged to have known him or watched him."

At the annual Loughborough past and present students v the AAA meeting a few weeks after the Paris air crash, the 1968 Olympic 400m hurdles champion, David Hemery ran a fast 200m hurdles as a tribute to John Cooper. Soon after his return from Tokyo, his father brought his two silver medals to the monthly meeting of the County Association. They were passed round in awe, for they represented a peak of effort by any Leicestershire athlete in the Olympic Games. He was buried in the village of Bitteswell, near Lutterworth, where he had been brought up, and there is a stained glass window in his memory in the Church.

Pat Cropper MBE (nee Lowe)

b.15.9.43
Belgrave United AC
Leicester CAT Birchfield
Harriers   800 m
XIX Olympic Games
Mexico City 1968
XX Olympic Games
Munich 1972

Pat Lowe of Leicester was so small, but so eager, that she was allowed to join Belgrave United AC under their lower age limit, subject to being approved after a period of probation. The club's headquarters, two rooms in a wooden hut, were bursting at the seams and its founder, teacher Reg Burton, worked like a trojan. The club had been given permission to use the Police Recreation Ground, Melton Road, by the Chief Constable, O.J.B. Cole. Sprints were organised by a football field, and as County Schools secretary - and still President in 1992 - Reg had his finger on the recruiting pulse.

Pat made her sprinting mark in the English Schools whilst attending Alderman Newton's School, finishing third in the 200 metres at Chesterfield in 26.5 secs. Belgrave eventually lost their ground and were amalgamated with Leicester Art and Tech. Later, when a student at Chelsea College of Physical Education, Pat joined Birchfield, and came under the coaching wing of Midland area coach, Bill Marlow.

In Leicestershire championships between 1962 and 1972, Pat won titles over all distances up to and including 800m and also excelled over 80m hurdles. Her championship best performance of 2-05.8 in 1971 has not been beaten. Pat adapted well to the demanding schedule of 800m training and made her GB debut in 1965 against West Germany on the first stage of the 3 x 800m relay.

The Olympics of 1968 began to loom and athletes became concerned about the perils of competing in Mexico City at an altitude of 7500 feet. A lot of the neurosis was dispersed by the report of the Medical Research Council which had been led by Dr L.G.C. Pugh and Dr Raymond Owen, backed by a fine team. Acclimatisation was one of the keys to running at such a height and this was taken on board by the athletics authorities.

Pat made her Olympic debut in heat three of the 800 metres, finishing third in 2-09.5 along with M. Dupareur (France) and D. Brown (USA), who were all given the same time. In the semi final, Pat again came third, in 2-06.6, going through to the ultimate test with M. Manning (USA) 2-05.8 and I. Silai (Rumania) 2-05.9. The other semi final was won by Maria Gomers (Netherlands) who had a world one mile record to her credit at Saffron Lane Stadium, Leicester.

Manning won the final in 2-00.9, with Sheila Taylor (GB) fourth in 2-03.8 and Pat again

Pat Cropper (50), nee Lowe . (E. D. Lacey)

lowering her time, sixth in 2-04.2. Pat was later to win several IAAF world record relay plaques, but there was only the sprint 4 x 100m for women in Mexico.

Looking to the Olympics at Munich in 1972, Pat, by then married to David Cropper (Birchfield), hoped to make it a twosome for the GB team, both over 800m metres. David, a member of Berry Hill, Mansfield, was well known in Leicester through his connections with the North Midlands cross country league. Pat had ended 1971 rated number one in the UK by Andrew Huxtable and Peter Matthews. A runner-up in the European 800m championship in 2-1.7, her top career mark, Pat aspired to make the Olympic final in Munich. Running in heat three Pat knew she had to get into the first three or be the fastest loser to get into the semis. She finished fourth in 2-03.5, the first lap having being run in 59.3. So that ended her Olympic career, and unfortunately her husband narrowly failed to qualify for the final.

Other distinctions in the Pat Cropper file include winning a Midland senior cross country title, competing in the IAAF championship and as a superb athlete with the baton, helping to set five world relay records. She also captained the British team and won a WAAA 800m title.

Brian Adams

b.13.3.49
British United AC
Leicester CAT Leicester
Walking Club
20 Kilometres Road Walk
XXI Olympic Games
Montreal 1976

Brian Adams, as an apprentice engineer at the British United Shoe Machinery Co., Leicester, originally began his sporting career as a cross country runner. From his father Peter, the County AAA President in 1992, he derived some appreciation of what was involved in competition. Later he took teacher training, taught in Leicester at Westcotes School and then moved to Sheffield, the hot bed of Northern Race Walking. A dedicated Christian with an understanding of young people, for several years he was race-walking team manager for Leicestershire Schools.

Undoubtedly his appearance in the 1976 Montreal Olympics, means an enormous amount to him. Brian's own description of how it felt to be walking in the Olympics makes very interesting reading and it reveals much about a man who has won the respect of fellow competitors across the world. In an account written especially for the author, he says:

"I remember using the 'running' clock in the stadium to check my pace over the two laps of the track (I didn't want to get carried away). This meant I was in 22nd position leaving the stadium. Many in front of me suffered on the long, steep climb from stadium to park, having gone off too fast. I gradually pulled through to 11th at 15km and held that to the end. It was very exciting entering the stadium to finish - I could enjoy this as there was no one to try and catch and no one to "hold off".

"My time 90.46 was a little disappointing, but relative to other walkers (I beat some good ones, for I was the first British walker) it was satisfactory. It was a good year to do the Olympics. After 1976 the standard of walking rocketed. Now, Phil Vesty's 87.20 doesn't get him in the top 20 in the World Championship....

"I was able to meet many athletes there who share my Christian faith, something that made me think again about the place Jesus has in my athletics.

"Walk with Jesus"

However, Brian Adams has succeeded at so many different levels that ranking him in any particular event is really a matter of personal choice. His successes include a personal best of 87-46 in the 20 km final in the Lugano World Cup in 1957, in which he ended sixth; five successive wins in the AAA 10,000m. between 1957 and 1979, including a Championship best of 42-40;

three successive victories in the Leicester Mercury Road Walk from 1977 - 1979; and first place in the National 100 km Championship in 1983.

In 1984 Brian also became Leicester's fastest 100-mile man, with a time on county roads from the New Parks to Bosworth area of 17 hrs. 39 mins. 28 sec. Brian Adams himself chose not to compete in the Moscow Olympics. "Many Christians and dissidents have been sent to prison by the Soviets", he said in the *Leicester Mercury* in May 1980, "so naturally it would be against my principles to compete".

Conrad Mainwaring

b.2.10.51 ANTIGUA
City of Leicester School
Leicester Coritanians
400m Hurdles
XXI Olympic Games
Montreal 1976

A brilliant all rounder, but too lightly built to have reached the top in the decathlon, Conrad Mainwaring also had many fine qualities as a potential first class coach. Born on October 2 1951, Conrad was 24 when he competed for Antigua in Montreal. A letter to the Antiguan AAA from the author confirmed his performances, and a delighted Conrad found himself in Montreal with another city athlete and Christian, the walking club's Brian Adams.

The Montreal Games was marred by the African boycott which meant that John Aki Bua, who had succeeded David Hemery to the Olympic 400m hurdles title, was not able to take part. However, a name to be blazoned around the world for the next decade or so emerged, that of Edwin Moses.

Conrad ran in heat three, which was won in 50.91 by M. Shine (USA). Conrad, sixth, clocked 54.67.

Sebastian Coe

b. 29.9.56
Hallamshire Harriers
Loughborough University
800m silver medallist (1980 & 1984)
1500m gold medallist (1980 & 1984)
XXII Olympic Games Moscow
XXIII Olympic Games Los Angeles

(George Herringshaw)

After winning gold and silver medals in Moscow in 1980, Sebastian Coe had to do it all over again in Los Angeles in 1984, bearing in mind that no athlete had ever retained a title in the men's 1500m.

His eventual haul of those four precious discs made him Britain's all-time most successful Olympic athlete. To climb the mountain he had to run four high quality races in the 800m and two in the 1500m. The pressure was enormous, posing great strain on health, endurance, stamina and mental competence.

An insight into these aspects was given by Coe himself. In the early 80's during the Dairygate sponsored series of meetings at Saffron Lane, he had seized on the word concentration, a key which received nodding approval from Loughborough guru, George Gandy. Herb Elliott, Australia's 1960 Olympic 1500m champion in Rome, earned praise from Coe as one of the greatest in the metric mile.

Coe lined up for the Los Angeles Olympic 800m final as the world record holder (1-41.73). His silver trail consisted of four races, in 1-45.71, 1-46.75, 1-45.51 and 1-43.64. In the 1500m final, Coe bolted from 200m from a strong tactical position and possessed the switch gear to fly home in 3-32.53, Steve Cram taking the silver in 3-33.40.

Now a member of Parliament, his shoes hung up,

he supports charity appeals in the county, staying with former Loughborough student and confidant, Steve Mitchell. Seb represented an era carved in granite in the history of world and local athletics. Shall we ever see his like again?

Philip Vesty

b.5.1.1963
Leicester Walking Club
20 Kilometres Walk
XXIII Olympic Games
Los Angeles 1984

When Phil Vesty of Leicester Walking Club won the UK 10km championship in 40 mins 53.60 secs. in a United Kingdom record time, his barometer seemed set for a fine Olympic year. That was in May 1984, and the Games in August could not come too soon for this hard grafting,

Philip Vesty (G. Herringshaw)

ambitious race-walker. Representing Britain in Los Angeles, USA, Vesty competed with distinction and was first man home for Britain, 13th, in 1 hr. 27 mins. 28 secs.. He was then only aged 21 years and could hopefully expect to take part in at least another couple of Games, especially Seoul, Korea, in 1988. To further his career and to be able to enjoy warm weather training throughout the winter, Vesty went to Australia, with a competitive spell in New Zealand. Unfortunately on his return he contracted a virus, his career was seriously undermined and so far he has never been the same brilliant athlete who was tasting stardom. The foundation stones had been laid perfectly on many roads and tracks at home and abroad. Regular outings in the English Schools Championships plotted a lot of his progress.

From a debut as a junior in 1976, finishing sixth in the 3 km, a year later Vesty won his first gold in 14-31. A National youths crown followed over 5 km in 22-50 in 1979. A disqualification in the All-England was a jolt and in this same year of the Moscow Olympics (1980), Phil finished 11th in the Olympic trial, over 20 km in 95-15. A junior international debut was most satisfying and 12 months later in 1981, on Braunstone Park, Leicester, Phil became the English Schools 10 km senior winner. Tackling the senior

AAA 3 km event, he set a British junior record of 12-17.96, taking second spot.

His senior international debut was against Italy, sixth in the 10 km in 45-30. Subsequently he lowered the British junior 3 km record to 12-02.04, and won the AAA under 20 UK championship over 10 km.

By 1983 he was good enough to challenge almost anyone in the country. He walked in the World Cup (Lugano Trophy) semi final and the final in Norway. Phil went to Canada for the World Student Games, came 11th in the 20 km and then journeyed to Helsinki, Finland, for the inaugural World Championships where he was 25th in 87-20.

Illness ruined a sparkling career, but he continues to take part in walking races, although in a much lower key.

Diana Davies

b.7.5.1961
Leicester Coritanians
High Jump
XXIII Olympic Games
Los Angeles 1984
XXIV Olympic Games
Seoul 1988

How many athletes who have not improved their personal best in ten years can claim to have competed in most of the major games and championships? That distinction belongs to Diana Davies. In Bislett Stadium, Oslo, June 26 1982, Diana, then Miss Elliott, momentarily held her breath and attacked the bar, soaring clear at 1.95m (6ft. 4 ¾ins.). For an athlete only 1.74m tall (5ft. 8 ½ins.), that was a superb jump. In vain, ever since, UK compatriots have tried but never done so well. That UK record has grown in stature with each passing year, defying all comers in an exceptionally long reign.

Born in Catworth, Cambridgeshire, Diana was recruited by Leicester Coritanians when living with her parents in Northampton, and it was for Northants that she achieved national recognition for the first time by winning an English Schools intermediate title with 1.73m in 1976. She retained her crown a year later with a championship best of 1.79m. She regularly made the 40 odd miles journey to Saffron Lane Stadium, Leicester, initially coached by Dave Lewis, teacher David Couling and for a long time now, national event coach, Malcolm Smith of Leicester. Most of her jumping routines are now done at Loughborough University where Malcolm runs a squad, a facility-granted privilege that is highly valued. Diana married former Royal Navy man Peter Davies, who holds the County championship best performance for 1500 metres of 3-48.2.

Daughter Laura was born in 1991, which meant a virtually competition free year for Diana. She now faces the prospect of a long haul back to the top, seeking the bounce, bound and elasticity of the golden year of the 1.95m. Diana failed in pursuit of a third Olympics place in Barcelona but there have been numerous highlights in her remarkable career. Since 1975 when she was 14, her best of the year is as follows: 1.55, 1.73, 1.79, 1.82, 1.75 (indoors), 1.83, 1.87, 1.95 - the UK record in 1982. Translated into championships, this is four each in the WAAA and United Kingdom, plus 50 international appearances.

She topped the British rankings between 1984-8 and in addition to that outdoor UK best set four indoor marks, the best being a record 1.94, equalled in 1991. She has twice competed in the Commonwealth Games, coming 6th and 4th, as well as

*Jack Buckner
(George Herringshaw)*

the European cup and championships, and also the World. Her biggest regret was narrowly missing a medal in the Edinburgh Commonwealth Games, but she can be justifiably elated at making two Olympic finals.

Jack Buckner
b. 22.9.61
Charnwood AC and Loughborough University.
5000m
XXIV   Olympic Games Seoul 1988
XXV   Olympic Games Barcelona 1992

When eventually a Hall of Fame is established for local sportsmen and women, the county senior cross country champion of 1985 will occupy an honoured spot. Let us briefly summarise his main achievements. They include the National 10,000m road championship in 1985; silver medal, 5000m Commonwealth Games and gold medal, 5000m European Championships in 1986; bronze medal, 5000m World Championships in 1987; and 6th in the 5000m, Seoul Olympics in 1988.

With the Commonwealth Games, the European and World Championships behind him, Jack made the Seoul Olympic final, after the bruising experience of waiting to see if he had qualified as a fastest loser. Chapter 14 of his book *Running the Distance* finds him in the stadium before the race, after a nerve-wracking journey, much of it spent stuck in a traffic jam. "Thirty minutes before an Olympic final I would be surprised if I experienced anything other than nervous fragility. It is time to report. Of the fifteen runners only five were finalists in last year's Rome World Championships, Domingos Castro, Sydney Maree, John Ngugi, Evgueni Ignatov and myself…There are 100,000 spectators attending but the noise and level of excitement is not as great as at many of the European meetings I have attended. I run a couple of strides along the back straight. It is reassuring to stretch out and move fluently after all the waiting…

"A moment of silent tension. Bang, I must conserve energy and do not compete for a position. When I am running well concentration becomes unnecessary until the end of the race…

"Ngugi has split the race apart…Nobody is catching Ngugi. I do not have the strength to lead the chase. I have battled into the first half dozen, John Doherty leads the race for second place until near 3000m when Domingo Castro takes over. Ngugi is six seconds ahead at 3000m. I thought Castro might chase Ngugi but he will not enjoy leading the pursuit. He does not like front running. If I could stay with Castro I could still have a chance of a medal. Castro is scampering away

from the second group, but I cannot chase him. My strength is fast ebbing away. My upper body is relaxed but I feel as if I am hauling my legs reluctantly around the track. My only hope is to keep plodding away…It is the last lap and I am left to chase Sydney Maree for fifth place. I close on him over the last 200m, but cannot overtake him. I cross the line dizzy and faint with exhaustion. Baumann is sprawled across the track. Ngugi is waving the Kenyan flag. Castro is crying. I stumble towards the changing rooms. It is all over. I feel empty, flat, vacant. I do not know what happens next. I have only thought about life up until the Olympic final. What happens now?…"

But at the end of the day, there is inspiration from Jack Buckner's self analysis - hope for all those who indulge themselves in a sport which often consists of activity between injuries.

Lisa York
b. 19.3.70
Leicester Coritanians
3000m
XXV Olympic Games
Barcelona 1992

As a young athlete there was very little in the way of top honours that Lisa York had not won. The first hallmark of potential future success in Leicestershire is often measured by performances in the Leicestershire Primary Schools Cross Country League.

The atmosphere is electric, the pressure to succeed immense, and in huge fields, taking control on the front indicates the presence of a special athlete. Lisa came through her apprenticeship with flying colours. She continued to develop her winter ability and was a key member of the club that triumphed in the team races of national younger age groups and on the road too.

After winning the WAAA intermediate 1500m in 1986, by 1989 at the age of 19 she had earned a 1500m senior international debut against Belgium and Cuba in Brussels, finishing third in a club record time of 4-15.7. In the European junior championships that season, Lisa took fifth places in the finals of the 1500 and 3000 metres. The year had begun at

Lisa York (G. Herringshaw)

Gateshead, when her stamina was taxed to its fullest in winning the Junior cross country trial for Britain's first team for the IAAF World Championships. In 1992 her cross country eminence peaked at Cheltenham when she won the Women's Senior National Cross Country title. That had been preceded by the second of her two wins in the Midland championships, and her Olympic year began to take on a meaningful look.

En route to the Olympic trial in Birmingham, Lisa had set a British indoors All-comers mile record in the National Indoor Centre of 4-33.50. There later came a magnificent run in Maderia, in a World Relay, where she ran a fastest leg, and was presented with an IAAF medal.

In the Women's 3000m championship at Birmingham's Alexander Stadium, fifty metres before the bell Lisa started a long run for home. She opened a gap on the Australian Krishna Stanton and produced two surges to reach her goal of National gold and Olympic selection. Her time of 8-50.18 was close to her personal best of 8-49.28.

In Barcelona, in her heat, Lisa had the guts to take on the field entering the final circuit. She got picked off ultimately by the American, who took third, and the last qualifying place, Patti Sue Plumer, who clocked 8-47.58. Lisa came in on 8-47.71. She had run in 29 degree heat and 89 per cent humidity, the kind of conditions seldom experienced in this country. "It didn't feel too bad at first", she recalled, "but by the fourth lap I started to eat my sweat and was gulping air." She had run a 62 seconds last lap, normally fast enough to take care of fierce opposition. But in the Olympics, with hindsight, and looking to the future Games in 1996, Lisa will hope to kick so hard she will be able to run a 60 seconds last lap, 28 seconds last 200.

Maxine Newman

b. 15.12.1970
Leicester Coritanians
1500m
XXV Olympic Games
Barcelona 1992

Leicester Coritanian Maxine Newman has often trod the same traditional route in Leicestershire to get to the top. Like Lisa York, most of her early development was done with the aid of Coritanian coach, John Price. Recently they parted company, after Maxine's packed log of successes included winning the Women's Inter Counties Intermediate cross country title, gold team medals in national road and cross country races, and a trip to Yugoslavia for the European junior 1500m championship, partnered by Lisa York, with whom she had run endless training sessions.

Maxine has the first

Maxine Newman
(George Herringshaw)

distinction of winning Midland Counties Cross Country titles across all the age groups, but the one race that stands out in her development was the English Schools senior 1500m gold won at Wigan in 1989. Superior tactics had to be employed to beat Natalie Tait, the fastest 800m age group runner that year. Maxine set a relentless pace, ensuring any sting which Tait would produce was going to be weakened. Newman held on for a still standing championship best performance of 4-17.1, and in the Olympic trial this was brought down after some years of hard work to just outside 4-10.

In Barcelona Maxine was eighth in her heat in 4-15.16, but at the age of 22 lives to fight another day.

APPENDIX 1: ROLL OF HONOUR

The increased number of fixtures, especially in the lower age groups has given numerous athletes the opportunities to compete in international competitions. Meetings billed as Home Countries, part of which is on an inter-area basis, are accepted as having a meaningful status. At the turn of the century international gatherings were few, many being for seniors only until the outbreak of World War Two in 1939. Schools internationals widened the scope and more recently even indoors competitions have come on stream.

Adams, Brian	20k walk	Ellway, Ruth	Road
Adams, Phil	Putting shot	Falkner, Ryan	Cross country
Allen, Claire	Cross/MD	Ford, Brian	100m
Allen, Neil	Cross country	Foster, Elaine	Cross country
Armitage, Andy	Cross country	Foster, Neil	Steeplechase
Atton, Karl	10k walk	Fox, Harold	800m
Barker, Matthew	MD	Frazer, Jennifer	High jump
Barratt, Tom	Putting shot	Frost, Helen	400m
Barry, Jim	Sprints	Gibbs, Brenda	High jump
Berwick, Chris	50k walk	Gillespie, Jim	400m hurdles
Blackburn, Peter	Long jump	Goddard, Bill	1500m
Boggis, John	3,000m	Gower, Peter	1500m
Bonsor, Alison	Hurdles	Green, Scott	Cross country
Bott, Jonathan	10k walk	Griffiths, Geraint	High jump
Buckner, Jack	5,000m	Grove, Ron	Road (marathon),
Butler, Derek	100m		track (10k) Cross C.
Caine, John	Cross country	Hames, Jeremy	Decathlon
Callan, Richard	5,000m	Harrison, Jennifer	High jump
Campbell, Mike	High jump	Hawes, Trevor	Ultra/marathon
Cartwright, Russell	800m	Heward-Mills, Rodney	Triple jump
Chamberlain, James	10k walk	Hibberd, Matthew	1500m
Chohan, Milimo	Hurdles	Higgins, Terry	400m
Christmas, Ruth	Cross country/800m	Johnson, Hilary	Ultra (100k)
Clarke, Peter	Putting shot	Johnson, Ken	Steeplechase
Clelland, Shirley	Pentathlon	Johnson, T. Lloyd	50k walk
Cobley, Don	Modern Pentathlon	Jones, Pat	Hurdles
Colledge, Louise	Hurdles	Kemp, Katrina	800m
Collis, Tim	100m	Kenney, Paul	Cross c./marathon
Cooper, John	400m h/relay	Khalifa, Omar	800m
Crofts, Andrea	5,000 walk	King, Alan	50k walk
Davies, Diana	High jump	Knowles, Martin	1500m
Davies, Pete	1500m	Lansdowne, Gill	High jump
Davis, Jackie	Marathon	Lem, David	Cross country
Denham, John	Steeplechase	Lowe, Pat	800/relays
Dodds, Matthew	Decathlon	Lynch, Andrew	High jump
Draper, Reg	Cross country	Maddocks, Alan	Cross Country
Dronfield, Jason	High jump	Mainwaring, Conrad	Hurdles
Duddle, Rosemary	Half marathon	Makepeace, Phil	Cross country
Edwards, Mark	Putting shot	Mallard, Karen	Discus

Markham, Peter	Vet walk	Ross, Fiona	High jump
Martin, Des	Cross country	Rushin, Phil	Hammer
Masterson, Joey	Marathon	Scutt, Steve	400m
Maycock, Tracy	Cross country	Shah, Arif	200m
McCaffrey, Nick	Cross country	Sheen, Rob	Road
McClelland, Jim	Cross country	Slater, Robert	1500m
McGeorge, Chris	800m	Smith, Chris	30k walk
McGeorge, Sonia	Cross country	Southam, Carl	400m/relay
Mills, Bobbie	Cross c./marathon	Stamatakis, Geoff	Hammer
Mochrie, Craig	Cross country	Tan, E.Y.	Triple jump
Monk, Chris	Sprints	Tancred, Bill	Discus
Morton, Glenys	Long jump	Taylor, Eric	15k walk
Moult, Chris	1500m	Taylor, Linden	Cross country
Newman, Maxine	Cross country/1500m	Thompson, Kevin	CC
Newton, Peter	Hammer	Thompson, Wilburt	400m
Nightingale, Danny	Modern Pentathlon	Titterington, Helen	10k
Norman, John	Walk	Tolley, Malcolm	10k walk
Norton, Nicholas	100m	Toone, Ron	Sprints
Nurse, Gary	Cross country/1500m	Trigg, Andy	50k walk
Offord, John	S/chase/marathon	Vesty, Phil	20k walk
O'Neill, Jean	Sprints	Vincent, John	10k walk
Paddick, John	20k walk	Wadeson, Bev	Putting shot
Payne, Dave	Cross country	West, Scott	Track/Cross country
Pen, Tony	Vet Cross country	Whetton, Karen	Cross country
Poynton, Fred	20 miles walk	Whitehead, Jim	Hammer
Pratt, Len	Vet triathlon	Wilkes, Melanie	Cross country
Pratt, Suzie	10k walk	Wilkinson, J.C.M.	Sprints
Ramsey, Kate	Cross country	Williams, Mike	Sprints
Raven, Mrs C	Cross country	Wray, Yvonne	Hurdles
Read, Peter	Long jump	Yardley, Malcolm	400m
Roscoe, Dennis	Discus	Yeoumans, Alfred	10 miles walk
Roscoe, Janet	400m	York, Lisa	3k/Road/Cross country

FOOTNOTE: Enderby-born Alfred Yeoumans, who represented his country in the 10 miles walk in the 1908 London Olympics, also won a total of 24 world records. However, he is probably better remembered for his feat in walking faster than the Swansea to Llanelly train in 1904.

APPENDIX 2: PROGRESSION OF LEICESTERSHIRE AND RUTLAND AAA CHAMPIONSHIP BEST PERFORMANCES

SENIOR MEN

100 YARDS
1919	H. Arrowsmith	LH	10.6
1927	W. Spencer	LH	10.4
1929	W. Spence	LH	10.2
1937	D. Richards	De Mont. AC	10.2
1949	R. Toone	L CAT	10.0
1967	J. Barry	Birchfield	10.0

100 METRES
1969	J. Barry	Verlea AC	10.8
1970	C. Monk	LC	10.6
1975	C. Monk	LC	10.6
1978	C. Monk	LC	10.6

220 YARDS
1924	T. Stevenson	LH	24.6
1927	W. Spencer	LH	23.6
1932	W. Spencer	LHs	23.2
1949	R. Toone	L.C.A.T.	22.5
1960	M. Yardley	Birchfield	22.3
1961	M. Yardley	Birchfield	22.2
1962	M. Yardley	Birchfield	22.2
1963	J. Barry	Man University	22.0
1967	J. Barry	Birchfield	21.7

200 METRES
1969	J. Barry	Verlea	22.4
1970	C. Monk	LC	22.2
1971	C. Monk	LC	21.6
1985	M. Williams	LC	21.4

440 YARDS
1920	J. W. Eaddy		54.4
1927	W. Spencer	LH	54.4
1930	W. Spencer	LH	53.4
1931	W. Spencer	LH	53.2
1938	Robert Scott	L'boro Coll.	52.0
1957	T. McDermott	Belgrave UAC	51.7
1959	M. Gray	LCAT	51.0
1962	M. Gray	LCAT	50.6
1964	M. Yardley	Walton A.C.	48.9

400 METRES
1969	J. Barry	Verlea A.C.	50.0
1970	Paul Walsh	LC	50.0
1972	Paul Walsh	LC	49.5
1983	M. Aylwin	LC	49.4
1984	S. Scutt	W'ton/Bilston	48.41

880 YARDS (800 metres after 1964)
1934	R. V. Draper	N'eaton H	2 01 .8
1954	A. Gale	Kibworth	1 59.3
1958	W. Goddard	Melton	1 57.5
1961	P. Davie	LCAT	1 53.1
1964	M. Kingman	LU	1 52.2
1971	M. Knowles	LC	1 54.6
1978	G. Nurse	B. Leys School	1 53.7
1982	B. Owen	LC	1 53.5
1984	S. Ward	C'wood AC	1 53.1

ONE MILE
1920	J. Hall	LH	4 50
1928	B. Brewin	LH	4 28.6
1932	R. Draper	N'eaton H	4 26.2
1934	R. Draper	N'eaton H	4 25
1951	K. Johnson	LCAT	4 25
1953	K. Johnson	LCAT	4 21
1957	W. Goddard	LH	4 17.6
1958	W. Goddard	Melton AC	4 16.5
1960	W. Goddard	Melton AC	4 14.2
1961	W. Goddard	Holwell Wks	4 13.8
1962	W. Goddard	Holwell Wks	4 11.2

1500 METRES
1969	D. Lem	LC	3 50.9
1977	M. Knowles	LC	3 50.8
1980	R. Callan	LC	3 49.9
1991	P. Davies	LC	3 48.2

THREE MILES
1947	D. Cobley	H TC	
1948	E. Boot	LCAT	16.14
1951	D. Cobley	HTC	15 20.3
1953	D. Cobley	HTC	15 11
1959	K. Wright	Derby	14 26.4
1960	A. Gale	Oakham/Kett.	14 24
1962	W. Goddard	Holwell Works	14 11.8
1964	J. Owen	LCAT	14 08.4
1966	R. Grove	LCAT	14 02.8
1967	D. Lem	LCAT	13 53.4
1968	R. Grove	LCAT	13 48.8

5000 METRES
1969	D. Lem	LC	14 18.6
1971	D. Lem	Birchfield	14 06.9
1979	R. Callan	LC	13 59.8

SIX MILES

1963	P. Leake	LCAT	29	36.4
1964	R. Grove	Holwell Wks	29	08.6
1965	R. Grove	LCAT	29	02.4
1966	R. Grove	LCAT	28	26.6
1967	R. Grove	LCAT	28	18.8

10,000 METRES

1969	R. Grove	LC	28	59.4

TWO MILES WALK

1923	F. Poynton	LH	14	50.4
1961	P. Markham	LWC	14	47
1962	P. Stapleford	LWC	14	29
1968	G. Toone	LWC	13	49.9

3000 METRES

1969	G. Toone	LWC	12	51
1974	G. Toone	LWC	12	20.8
1975	B. Adams	LWC	12	18.2
1976	B. Adams	LWC	12	09.6
1984	P. Vesty	LWC	11	28.84

UK record, not ratified, short of qualified officials

120 YARDS HURDLES

1948	T. Barratt	LCAT/P. Jets	18.4
1949	J. Marshal	LH	18.0
1960	M. Hobday	Ratcliffe Coll.	17.01
1967	C. Brand	LCAT	15.0

110 METRES HURDLES

1969	T. Scott	L'boro Coll	15.2
1978	D. Hall	S. Wig. Coll	15.0

220 YARDS HURDLES

1961	J. Cooper	L'boro Coll	24.7

440 YARDS HURDLES (400 m from 1974)

1954	G. Thirlby	LH	60.4
1956	P. Brearley	L'boro Coll	59.8
1959	C. Turner	Kett. TH	57.8
1961	J. Cooper	L'boro Coll	57.4
1963	J. Hasdell	Leic Univ	56.9
1974	C. Shaw	LC	56.8
1981	D. Hall	LC	53.6

3000m METRES STEEPLECHASE

1967	P. Leake	LCAT	9	28.2
1968	J. Offord	LCAT	9	22.4
1973	M. Knowles	LC	9	17.7
1982	S. Bird	Leic Univ	9	09.4
1983	S. Bird	Leic Univ	9	04

HIGH JUMP

1927	E. Welton	LH	1.65
1928	E. Welton	LH	1.73
1948	R. Collett	LH	1.78
1949	R. Collett	LH	1.78
1951	R. Collett	LH	1.78
1952	D. Rodgers	LCAT	1.80
1963	C. Brand	LCAT	1.80
1965	C. Brand	LCAT	1.85
1966	C. Brand	LCAT	1.89
1971	D. Phillips	L'boro Coll	1.90
1978	G. Vorgic	C'wood	1.98
1990	J. Dronfield	LC	2.0
1991	A. Lynch	LC	2.06
1993	A. Lynch	LC	2.11

LONG JUMP

1946	R. Tate	LH	5.73
1947	T. Barratt	LCAT	6.17
1949	R. Tate	LH	6.27
1953	B. Weaver	LH	6.33
1956	W. Buckley	LH	6.39
1957	W. Buckley	Southend AC	6.46
1959	E. Dediare	Nigeria/L'boro C	6.53
1961	R. Cooper	Lutterworth GS	6.61
1963	R. Cooper	Hull University	6.61
1967	C. Brand	LCAT	6.97
1989	A. Starbuck	C'wood AC	7.14

HOP, STEP, JUMP/TRIPLE JUMP

1955	R. Beeby	LCAT	12.77
1957	R. Beeby	LCAT	13.08
1958	E. Y. Tan	S'pore/L'boro C	14.58

POLE VAULT

1954	W. Cunningham	Belg UAC	2.44
1955	A. Scott	LCAT	2.90
1964	C. Brand	LCAT	3.43
1965	R. Czerniawski	Oxford Univ	3.66
1967	C. Brand	LCAT	3.88
1984	R. Gamage	L'boro Univ	4.90

SHOT PUT

1946	T. Barratt	LCAT	12.33
1949	T. Barratt	LCAT	13.75
1964	M. Meade	Police	14.25
1971	D. Roscoe	TVH	15.20
1973	W. Tancred	Birchfield	17.97

DISCUS

1947	T. Barratt	LCAT	36.83
1948	T. Barratt	LCAT	37.83
1949	T. Barratt	LCAT	39.69

1954	F. Laudobellis	LCAT	40.84
1957	F. Laudobellis	LCAT	42.85
1959	F. Laudobellis	LCAT	44.26
1971	W. Tancred	Birchfield	55.98
1973	W. Tancred	Birchfield	59.86

JAVELIN
1946	T. Barratt	LCAT	50.43
1957	J. Watson	Hinckley GS	52.10
1958	J. Watson	Belgrave UAC	56.16
1970	H. Ferrary	L'boro' Coll	68.88

New Specifications
1987	N. Waring	LC	51.60
1993	A. Holloway	C'wood	62.0

HAMMER
1957	P. Bramley	Anstey/RAF	43.56
1965	J. Goodban	L'boro Coll	46.99
1972	J. Whitehead	Birchfield	53.06
1973	J. Whitehead	Birchfield	58.94

WOMEN
100 YARDS
1938	B. Stapleford	College of Arts	12.1
1948	B. Schofield	LCAT	11.7
1949	B. Schofield	LCAT	11.5
1951	J. Giblett	LH	11.4
		Heat	11.3
1952	M. Parker	LCAT	11.3
1967	W. Walker	Birchfield	11.1
1968	J. O'Neill	LCAT	10.8

100 METRES
1969	J. O'Neill	Bedford CPE	12.2
1970	J. O'Neill	Bedford CPE	11.8

220 YARDS
1948	J. Morgan	LCAT	28.5
1949	J. Morgan	LCAT	27.8
1952	M. Parker	LCAT	27.3
1956	B. Burbidge	LH	27.3
1958	J. Snow	LH	27.0
1960	J. Snow	Melton AC	26.6
1961	B. Burbidge	Leic YMCAH	26.4
			(heat)
1966	W. Walker	Birchfield	26.2
1967	J. O'Neill	Lutterworth GS	24.8
1968	J. O'Neill	LCAT	24.4

200 METRES
1970	J. O'Neill	Bedford CPE	25.0
1972	J. Roscoe	Stretford AC	24.3

440 YARDS
1954	M. Redhead	Belgrave UAC	68.8
1955	J. Phillips	Belgrave UAC	67.9
1958	B. Burbidge	Leic YMCAH	66.7
1960	B. Burbidge	Leic YMCAH	65.7
1961	B. Burbidge	Leic YMCAH	64.5
1962	P. Lowe	LCAT	61.2
1963	P. Lowe	LCAT	60.4
1966	P. Lowe	Birchfield	58.8
1967	P. Lowe	Birchfield	57.8

400 METRES
1973	J. Roscoe	Stretford	56.1

800 METRES
1969	P. Lowe	Birchfield	2 7.8
1971	P. Lowe	Birchfield	2 5.8

1500 METRES
1974	C. Helsby	Scraptoft College	5 32.4
1977	K. Butters	LC	5 00.4
1978	D. Curtis	J Cleveland Coll	4 51.1
1980	J. Burtonwood	LC	4 41.4
1981	J. Burtonwood	LC	4 40.2
1988	E. Foster	C'wood AC	4 29.5

3000 METRES
1981	J. Burtonwood	LC	10 05.3
1984	B. Everley	Leic Univ	9 53.6
1988	E. Foster	C'wood AC	9 38.4
1989	R. Mackay	LC	9 35.5

80 METRES HURDLES
1948	P. Vines	LCAT	14.4
1951	B. Moffatt	LH	13.0
1953	B. Moffatt	LH	12.9
1967	S. Slattery	LCAT	12.2
1968	P. Jones	Leic Univ	11.1

100 METRES HURDLES
1969	S. Clelland	LC	15.3
1970	S. Clelland	Dartford CPE	14.3

400 METRES HURDLES
1984	L. Brown	C''wood AC	70.4

HIGH JUMP
1949	M. Avis	Morris Sports	1.43
1951	M. Avis	Morris Sports	1.52
1954	J. Frazer	LH	1.52
1967	A. Hunt	Belg UAC	1.52
1972	G. Lansdowne	LC	1.58
1974	G. Lansdowne	LC	1.62

1975	J. Harrison	LC	1.68
1978	B. Gibbs	LC	1.74
1980	B. Gibbs	LC	1.75
1985	D. Davies	LC	1.80

LONG JUMP

1951	B. Patrick	LH	4.09
1952	M. Parker	LCAT	4.77
1953	B. Patrick	LH	5.08
1954	E. Campbell	Belg UAC	5.19
1960	Y. Haywood	Rawlins GS	5.20
1963	Y. Haywood	Bedford CPE	5.25
1966	S. Clelland	L'boro Coll Sch	5.27
1967	S. Clelland	L'boro Coll Sch	5.26
1968	S. Clelland	L'boro Coll Sch	6.08
1981	G. Morton	LC	6.26

SHOT PUT

1955	M. Cox	Belg UAC	8.79
1958	J. Hyman	LCAT	9.07
1959	J. Hyman	LCAT	9.73
1966	J. Denton	LCAT	9.98
1968	P. Jones	Leic Univ/Bfd	10.99

1969	P. Jones	Birchfield	11.34
1970	P. Jones	Birchfield	12.38

DISCUS

1954	J. Hyman	Belg UAC	29.46
1956	J. Hyman	Coventry TC	35.84
1959	J. Hyman	LCAT	36.70
1975	K. Mallard	LC	40.02
1986	R. Hardy	Charnwood	40.04

JAVELIN

1962	C. Muggleton	LCAT	32.82
1971	R. Withers	LC	34.56
1972	B. Withers	LC	38.58
1975	S. Hallam	LC	40.70
1978	S. Hallam	LC	41.75

HAMMER

| 1993 | C. Hardy | Charnwood | 26.66 |

APPENDIX 3: LOCAL WINNERS OF MIDLAND SENIOR CHAMPIONSHIPS

100 YARDS/100 METRES

1897	George F. Brewill	Loughborough AC	10.0 Y
1899	George F. Brewill	Loughborough AC	10.0
1947	Ronald Toone	Morris Sports	10.3
1970	Chris Monk	Coritanians	10.8 M
1971	Chris Monk	Coritanians	10.9
1973	Chris Monk	Coritanians	10.5
1976	Chris Monk	Coritanians	10.9
1977	Chris Monk	Coritanians	10.7

200 YARDS/200 METRES

1897	George F. Brewill	Loughborough AC	23.0 Y
1899	George F. Brewill	Loughborough AC	23.4
1901	George F. Brewill	Loughborough AC	23.8
1948	Ronald Toone	Leicester CAT	23.8 M
1963	Jim Barry	Birstall/Birchfield	22.4
1965	Jim Barry	Birstall/Birchfield	22.4
1966	Jim Barry	Birstall/Birchfield	22.7
1970	Chris Monk	Coritanians	22.5
1973	Chris Monk	Birstall/Birchfield	21.5
1976	Chris Monk	Birstall/Birchfield	21.6
1977	Chris Monk	Birstall/Birchfield	21.6

440 YARDS/400 METRES

1896	Fred Cox	Leics. C & AC	54.8 Y
1898	Fred Cox	Leics. C & AC	53.4 Y
1934	Robert Scott	Ashby G.S.	52.6
1964	John Cooper	Lutt./Belg AC/Birchfield	49.0
1965	John Cooper	Lutt./Belg AC/Birchfield	48.5

800 METRES

| 1980 | Omar Khalifa | C'wood/Sudan | 1-52.7 |

ONE MILE/1500m (from 1992)

1953	Ken Johnson	LCAT	4-20.2
1955	Ken Johnson	LCAT	4-15.4
1958	Bill Goddard	Melton	4-17.2
1959	Bill Goddard	LH	4-19.8
1960	Bill Goddard	LH	4-13.0
1962	Bill Goddard	LH	4-09.7
1992	Pete Davies	LC	3-48.28

5000 METRES

1969	Dave Lem	LCAT/Bfd	14-12.4
1979	Dick Callan	LC	14-02
1981	Dick Callan	LC	13-59.50
1988	Craig Mochrie	LC	13-44.92 (CBP)

6 MILES/10,000m (from 1972)

1947	Reg Draper	HTC	30-34
1972	Dave Lem	LC	29-32
1990	Andrew Hart	LC	31-35.8

10 MILES

| 1968 | Ron Grove | LCAT | 48-21 |
| 1969 | Ron Grove | LC | 47-28.2 |

120 YARDS/110m HURDLES

| 1947 | R. P. Bird | LCAT | 17.1 Y |
| 1965 | Dave Barrington | LCAT | 15.6 |

220 YARDS HURDLES

| 1961 | John Cooper | L'boro C | 24.9 |
| 1962 | John Cooper | L'boro C | 25.0 |

440 YARDS/400m HURDLES

1949	Richard Collett	LH	59.5 Y
1954	George Thirlby	LH	57.0
1955	George Thirlby	LH	57.0
1961	John Cooper	L'boro/Bfd	54.8
1962	John Cooper	L'boro/Bfd	54.0
1967	John Cooper	L'boro/Bfd	53.0
1968	John Cooper	L'boro/Bfd	52.7
			(CBP)

MARATHON

1955	Brian Ashwell	LH	2-43.10
1968	Ron Grove	LCAT	2-20.22
1969	Ron Grove	LCAT	2-23.03

TWO MILES/3,000m STEEPLECHASE (from 1955)

1952	Ken Johnson	LCAT	10-28
1953	Ken Johnson	LCAT	10-12.4
1954	Ken Johnson	LCAT	10-13.2
1955	Ken Johnson	LCAT	9-24.2
1957	Ken Johnson	LCAT	9-19.6
1973	John Offord	LC	8-50.6

HIGH JUMP

1930	Albert Hardy	LH	1.65m
			(tied)
1954	David Rodgers	LCAT	1.80m
1956	Michael Day	Racliffe College	1.83m
1957	Michael Day	Racliffe College	1.78m
1969	Colin Brand	LCAT	1.84m
1990	Jason Dronfield	LC	2.06m
1991	Jason Dronfield	LC	1.90m
1992	Andrew Lynch	LC	2.06m

LONG JUMP

| 1955 | A. Buckley | LH | 6.68m |

TRIPLE JUMP

| 1972 | R. Spinks | LC | 14.70m |

POLE VAULT

1966	Colin Brand	LCAT	3.50m
1967	Colin Brand	LCAT	3.50m
1969	Colin Brand	LCAT	3.71m
1984	Richard Gammage	L'boro Uni	4.85m
1985	Richard Gammage	L'boro Uni	4.81m

SHOT PUT

1946	Tom Barratt	Power Jets LCAT	12.11m
1947	Tom Barratt	NGTE	12.21m
1948	Tom Barratt	NGTE	12.54m
1949	Tom Barratt	NGTE	13.0m
1950	Tom Barratt	NGTE	13.23m
1951	Tom Barratt	NGTE	12.83m
1952	Tom Barratt	NGTE	12.66m
1953	Tom Pukits	LCAT	13.94m
1954	Tom Pukits	LCAT	14.10m
1955	Fritz Laudobelis	LCAT	12.29m
1990	Phil Adams	LC	14.50m
1991	Phil Adams	LC	14.52m
1992	Phil Adams	Sale	15.57m

DISCUS (Jun Weight from 1946)

1920	W.H. Gray	LH	25.68m
1935	E.G. Ackhurst	L'boro C	37.76m
1946	Tom Barratt	NGTE	45.36m
1947	Tom Barratt	NGTE	36.48m
1948	Tom Barratt	NGTE	38.94m
1949	Tom Barratt	NGTE	39.52m
1950	Tom Barratt	NGTE	40.06m
1951	Tom Barratt	NGTE	39.62m
1952	Tom Barratt	NGTE	37.46m
1953	Fritz Laudbolis	LCAT	39.42m
1954	Tom Barratt	NGTE	39.44m

JAVELIN

1951	Tom Barratt	NGTE	55.04m
1969	Steve Ginns	Police	53.57m
1974	Jeff Hills	LC	52.07m

HAMMER

1908	R.S. Cole	Police	21.18m
1920	W.H. Gray	LH	23.54m
1922	J.R. Capps	LFGC	23.66m
1988	Phil Rushin	LC	57.50m

APPENDIX 4: GREAT LOCAL TRACK AND FIELD PERFORMANCES

MEN

Year	Event	Name	Club	Mark
1973	100m	C Monk	LC	10.4
1973	200m	C Monk	LC	20.70
1992	400m	C Southam	LC	46.59
1991	800m	C McGeorge	L'boro	1-45.15
1983		O Khalifa	CH	1-45.3
1991		M Barker	LC	1-48.33
1986	1500m	J Buckner	CH	3-35.20
1987		C Mochrie	LC	3-41.0
1984	Mile	J Buckner	CH	3-51.57
1989		C Mochrie	LC	3-59.6
1986	3000m	J Buckner	CH	7-40.43
1983		D Callan	LC	7-47.56
1986	5000m	J Buckner	CH	13-10.15
1989		C Mochrie	LC	13-26.74
1982	10,000m	A Royle	Prior CH	27-14.16
1969		J Caine	LC	28-41.8
		R Grove	LC	28-51
1973	3000m S.Ch.	J Offord	LC	8-43.8
1968	10 miles	R Grove	LCAT	47-02.2
1968	One Hr	R Grove	LCAT	20,303m
1993	H jump	A Lynch	LC	2.16m
1990		J Dronfield	LC	2.08m
1973	L jump	P Blackburn	LC	7.44m
1973	Tr jump	P Blackburn	LC	15.77m
1985	P Vault	A Main	CH	4.30m
1969	Shot	W Tancred	L'boro	17.88m
1974	Discus	W Tancred	L'boro	64.94m
1989	Javelin	A Holloway	CH	67.72m
1979	Hammer	J Whitehead	Bfd	69.52m
1988		P Rushin	LC	59.10
1993	110m hurdles	P Donovan	LC	14.13
1964	400m hurdles	J Cooper	Bfd	50.1

WOMEN

Year	Event	Name	Club	Mark
1983	100m	A Inniss	LC	11.6
1984	200m	A Inniss	LC	24.0
1992	400m	H Frost (J)	LC	54.32
1971	800m	P Lowe	Bfd	2-01.7
1992	1500m	L York	LC	4-09.26
1992	Mile	L York	LC	4-27.80
1992	3000m	L York	LC	8-47.71
1989	5000m	H Titterington	LC	15-40.14
1992		E Foster	CH	16-09.83
1989	10,000m	H Titterington	LC	32-36.09
1985	100m hdls	D. Davies	LC	14.54
1988		C. Lockton	CH	14.6
1991	300m hdls	Helen Frost	LC	43.9
1981	400m hdls	Yvonne Wray	Scraptoft	54.46
1989		Helen Frost	LC	63.0
1982	High jump	Diana Davies	LC	1.95m
1981	Long jump	Glenys Morton	LC	6.33m
1991	Shot	Emma Spencer	LC	13.04m
1973	Discus	Karen Mallard	LC	43.24m
1974	Javelin	Sue Hallam	LC	42.88m
1985	Pentath.	D. Davies	LC	4794
	1600m relay:	Chambers, Wilkes, York, Kemp	LC	3-53.2

APPENDIX 5: ENGLISH SCHOOLS CHAMPIONSHIPS GOLDS

YEAR	GROUP	EVENT	NAME	SCHOOL	METRES/MIN/SEC
1931	B U 14	Long jump	A. Adcock	Old British Melton	5.0
1939	B U 14	220 yds	H. Branston	L'boro GS	25.3
1939	B 14-16	100 yds	S. Smith	Wyggeston GS	10.7
1939	B 14-16	220 yds	R. Ball	L'boro GS	24.2
1939	B 14-16	440 yds	R. Hutchins	Gateway	55.8
1946	B 14-16	440 yds	L. Clemerson	L'boro GS	53.2
1946	G 14-16	High jump	M. Avis	L'boro HS	1.45
1947	B U 14	880 yds	R. Brown	Westfield	2 16.5
1947	B U 14	Shot	C. Radford	Coalville	12.40
1948	J B	Shot	C. Radford	Coalville	12.0
1950	S G	Relay	County		53.8
			M. Dudley	Hinckley GS	
			C. Kirton	Ald. Newton	
			K. McNaughton	Hinckley GS	
			H.Simpson		
1951	J B	440 yds	P. Hollis	S. Wigston	54.0
1951	J B	Long jump	J. Allen	L'boro Coll Sch	5.97
1951	I G	High jump	J. Harvey	Ald. Newton	1.47
1952	J B	High jump	D. Robinson	Lutterworth	1.50
1952	I G	Long jump	I. Granger	S. Wigston	4.81
1952	S G	220 yds	M. Dudley	Hinckley GS	27.9
1953	I B	Discus	J. Waldron	Ashby GS	47.80
1953	I G	Discus	J. Hyman	H. Perkins	29.59
1953	S B	High jump	R. Warren	L'boro Coll'	1.75
1954	J B	Shot	P. Marsden	Linwood	13.69
1955	I B	High jump	B. Bouskill	Melton GS	1.80
1956	I B	440 yds	M. Yardley	Ald. Newton	51.4
1956	S G	High jump	J. Frazer	Wyggeston GS	1.56
1957	I B	440 yds	M. Yardley	Ald. Newton	50.8
1957	I B	Hop, step, jump	J. Cooper	Lutterworth GS	13.13
1961	I B	100 yds	N. Noton	Oakham	10.2
1968	S G	220 yds	J. O'Neill	Lutterworth	27.4
1968	J B	Discus	S. Yates		42.95
1969	S G	Long jump	S. Clelland	L'boro Coll' Sch	5.90
1970	S B	100m	C. Monk	Oadby Beauchamp	11.1
1971	J G	Long jump	J. Sanderson	Harborough GS	5.31
1971	J G	Shot	B. Wadeson	Newarke	11.04
1971	S B	440 yds hdles	G. Wood	Uppingham	53.9
1974	J B	100m	B. Ford	Enderby	11.5
1974	J B	1500m	R. Slater	Garendon	4.15.5
1975	J B	100m	D. Butler	Soar Valley	11.8
1975	J B	1500m	C. Moult	Ashby GS	4 12.3
1975	S B	5000	R. Callan	Harborough GS	14 40
1977	J G	Discus	S. Holwell	Stonehill	36.44
1979	I B	400m hdls	J. Gillespien	Melton GS CBP	55.66
1984	J G	Long jump	N. Goddard	Uppingham VC	5.42
1987	J B	80m hdles	M. Chona	Ratcliffe Coll'	11.4
1987	I G	1500m	M. Newman	L'boro Coll'	4 33.3

1988	J B	High jump	A. Lynch	Oadby Beauchamp	1.92
					(CBP)
1989	S B	800m	P. Burgess	Loughborough TC	1 48.6
					(CBP)
1989	J G	1500m	C. Allen	S. Wigston	4 29
1989	S G	1500m	M. Newman	L'boro Coll'	4 17.1
					(CBP)
1990	J B	1500m	S. West	Lutterworth GS	4 13.1
1990	S B	800m	M. Hibberd	Longslade	1 53.4
1990	S B	Shot	P. Adams	Countesthorpe C	16.32
1991	I B	Shot	M. Edwards	Burleigh CC	16.84
1991	S B	3000m	D. Robinson	Loughboro' TC	8 30.24
1992	S B	400m	C. Southam	Charles Keene C	47.28
1992	S B	1500m	M. Hibberd	Charles Keene C	3 51.10
1992	I B	1500m	S. West	Lutterworth GS	3 59.9
1992	J B	800m	R. Cartwright	Hastings	2 03.23
1992	S G	400m	H. Frost	Charles Keene C	55.73
1993	J B	200	A. Shah	Earl Shilton	22.93
1993	I G	80H	L. Colledge	Leicester H S	11.4

APPENDIX 6: SAFFRON LANE SPORTS CENTRE GROUND RECORDS

MEN

1970	100m	Ian Green	Yorks	10.4
1970	200m	Martin Reynolds	Middlesex	20.9
1982		Allan Wells	Edinburgh S. H.	20.9
1983		Luke Watson	Middlesex	20.9
1981	300m	David Jenkins	Gateshead	32.9
1980	400m	Steve Scutt	W & B	46.5
1970	800m	John Davies	Cheshire	1 48.8
1981	1000m	Seb Coe	L'boro' Univ	2 17.6
1968	1500m	John Boulter	South	3 44.9
1970	2000m	Kip Keino	Kenya	5 05.2
1971	Mile	Walter Wilkinson	Yorks	3 56.6
1968	2 miles	Lachie Stewart	Scotland	8 45.8
1982	3000m	Alan Mottershead	Stretford	8 00.4
1970	5000m	David Black	Staffs	13 46.2
1968	6 miles	Ron Grove	Leic. CAT	28 21.4
1971	10,000	Mike Freary	Lancs	28 33
1968	10 miles	Ron Hill	Bolton (World record April)	47 2.2
1968		Ron Hill	(World record November)	46 44
1968	one hour	Ron Hill	Bolton (C'wealth, All comers)	12 miles 1268 yds

WALKS NATIONAL RECORDS

1982	One mile	Phil Vesty	LWC	6 9.2
1984	3000m	Phil Vesty	LWC (UK record, not ratified)	11 28.4
1974	10,000	Raul Gonzales	Mexico	41 59
1969	24 hours	Colin Young	Essex	129 miles 115 yds
1969	100 miles	Colin Young	Essex	17hr 52min 32secs

WALKS

1982	One mile	Phil Vesty	Leicester	6 09.2
1984	3,000m	Phil Vesty	Leicester (UK record, not ratifield)	11 28.4
1974	10,000m	Raul Gonzales	Mexico	41 59
1972	20 miles	Paul Nihill	Surrey	2 40 42.6
1969	24 hours	Colin Young	Essex	129 miles 1,155 yds
1969	100 miles	Colin Young	Essex	17 hrs 52 mins 32 secs
1972	3,000m S/Chase	Steve Hollins	Yorks	8.39
1972	110m hurdles	Alan Pascoe	Hants	13.9
1971	400m hurdles	John Sherwood	Yorks	51.2
1968	4 X 100m relay		Wales	41.8
1967	Mile Medley relay			3 32.6
1981	High jump	Milton Goode	USA	2.19m
1972	Long jump	Allan Lerwill	QPH	8.15m
1982	Triple jump	Keith Connor	S. Maryland Univ., USA	16.39m
1982	Triple jump	Aston Moore	Birchfield	16.39m
1983	Pole vault	Geoff Gutteridge	Windsor	5.20m
1977	Shot	Geoff Capes	Enfield	20.99m
1973	Discus	Bill Tancred	L'boro U	59.86m
1983	Javelin	Roald Bradstock	Herts	85.26m
1980	Hammer	Karl Hans-Riehm	West Germany (All Comers record)	77.02m
1971	Decathlon	Peter Gabbett	Royal Navy	7,639

WOMEN

1983	100m	Lynn Parry	Derby	11.5
1985		Kathy Cook	W/Bilston	11.5
1989	200m	Phyliss-Watt Smith	W/Bilston	23.7
1982	300m	Michelle Scutt	Sale	36.33
1980	400m	Michelle Probert	Wales	51.62
1971	800m	Joan Allison	Cambridge	2 04.8
1972	1500m	Sheila Carey	Coventry	4 21.1
1969	One mile	Mia Gomers	Holland (World record)	4 36.8
1980		Christina Boxer	Aldershot	4 35.2
1981	3000m	Kathie Binns	Sale	9 20.3
1971	100m H	Ann Wilson	Southend	13.8
1983		Kerry Robin Miller-Chip	Bfd	13.8
1992	400m H	Gowry Retchakan	Thurrock	57.2
1981	High jump	Ann Marie Cording	Bedford	1.88m
1970	Long jump	Moira Walls	Western	6.36m
1987	Shot	Judy Oakes	Croydon (Nat league record)	18.37m
1970	Discus	Rosemary Payne	Bfd	52.94m
1987	Javelin	Tessa Sanderson	Hounslow	67.86m
1970	Pentathlon	Shirley Clelland	LCAT	4320
1973	4 X 100m		Stretford	48.2
1970	4 X 400m	National junior team Mary Somner, Jennifer Honick Elaine Saunders, Dawn Webster		3-47.8

WALKS

1983	5000m	Sally Pierson	Australia (Commonwealth record)	22-34
1983	10,000m	Sue Cook	Australia (World record)	45-47

APPENDIX 7: LEICESTER MERCURY WALK WINNERS

20 Miles

Year	Name	Club	Time
1927	T. Lloyd Johnson	Surrey	3-1-07
1928	T. Lloyd Johnson	Leicester	2-51-18
1929	T. Lloyd Johnson	Leicester	2-53-42
1930	T. Lloyd Johnson	Leicester	2-52-27
1931	Stan Smith	Derby	2-57-10
1932	Tommy Green	Belgrave	2-55-52
1933	John Wilson	Sheffield	2-52-08
1934	T.L. Johnson	Leicester	2-52-39
1935	Henry Hake	Surrey	2-49-17
1936	T.L. Johnson	Leicester	2-52-17
1937	Stan Fletcher	Derby	2-52-03
1938	Stan Fletcher	Derby	2-46-35
1939	Albert Staines	Leicester	2-53-48
1947	Harry Forbes	Birmingham	2-55-14
1948	T.L. Johnson	Leicester	3-00-40
1949	T.L. Johnson	Leicester	3-00-07
1950	John Proctor	Sheffield	2-53-24
1951	T.L. Johnson	Leicester	2-57-48
1952	John Proctor	Sheffield	2-59-55
1953	Frank Bailey	London Poly	2-59-41
1954	Roland Hardy	Sheffield	2-50-06
1955	Albert Johnson	Sheffield	2-52-36
1956	Albert Johnson	Sheffield	2-50-01
1957	Eric Hall	Belgrave	2-51-00
1958	Tommy Misson	Metropolitan	2-46-30
1959	Don Thompson	Metropolitan	2-49-56
1960	Tommy Misson	Metropolitan	2-46-05
1961	Pete Markham	Leicester	2-52-25
1962	Don Thompson	Metro'	2-45-58
1963	Vaughan Thomas	Belgrave	2-54-52
1964	Ray Middleton	Belgrave	2-51-41
1965	Peter McCullagh	Metro'	2-53-51
1966	Peter McCullagh	Metro'	2-41-22
1967	Rev. Roy Lodge	R.S. Coldfield	2-52-29
1968	Bryan Eley	Bristol	2-41-22
1969	Bryan Eley	Bristol	2-42-15
1970	Ron Wallwork	Lancs	2-37-22
1971	Shaun Lightman	Metro'	2-38-16
1972	Carl Lawton	Belgrave	2-39-39
1973	John Moullin	Belgrave	2-45-59
1974	Carl Lawton	Belgrave	2-35-36
1975	Shaun Lightman	Metro'	2-39-53
1976	Daniel Bautista	Mexico (World Best)	2-22-53
1977	Brian Adams	Leicester	2-34-45
1978	Brian Adams	Leicester	2-39-44
1979	Brian Adams	Leicester	2-37-35
1980	Amos Seddon	Enfield	2-31-33
1981	Alan King	Leicester	2-39-07
1982	Alan King	Leicester	2-43-26
1983	Murray Lambdon	Isle of Man	2-39-41
1984	Graham Seatter	Belgrave/NZ	2-26-56
1985	Murray Day	Belgrave/NZ	2-35-27

30 Kilometres

Year	Name	Club	Time
1986	Simon Moore	Leicester	2-22-26
1987	Les Morton	Sheffield	2-23-17
1988	Ray Hankin	Sheffield	2-28-45
1989	Les Morton	Sheffield	2-27-20

20 Kilometres

Year	Name	Club	Time
1990	Gareth Holloway	Splott	92-40
1991	Martin Rush	Lakeland	90-15

10 Kilometres

Year	Name	Club	Time
1992	Les Morton	Sheffield	43-48
1993	Chris Smith	Leicester	47-01

**APPENDIX 8: LOUGHBOROUGH STUDENTS PAST AND PRESENT VERSUS AAA
MEETING RECORDS AFTER 35th ANNUAL MATCH JUNE 20 1993**

The annual meeting between Loughborough students past and present and the AAA is the most prestigious in the country. Many Leicester athletes have competed in it, and no history of local athletics would be complete without this summary of meeting records.

1984	100m	P. Narracott	Australia	10.42
1984	200m	T. Bennett	AAA	20.73
1962	400m	R. Brightwell	LSAC	46.2
1980	800m	S. Coe	"	1 45.0
1986	1500m	J. Buckner	"	3 38.19
1986	3000m	T. Hutchens	"	7 44.88
1984	110m H	D. Wright	Australia	13.89
1993	400m H	P. Crampton	AAA	50.70
1981	3k S.Ch	D. Lewis	LSAC	8 38.30
1992	High jump	S. Smith	AAA	2.24
1986	Long jump	D. Brown	AAA	8.12
1984	Triple jump	J. Herbert	AAA	16.77
1989	Pole vault	M. Edwards	AAA	5.26
1980	Shot	G. Capes	AAA	21.35
1974	Discus	W. Tancred	LSAC	62.38
1991	Javelin	G. Lovegrove	Guest	80.48
1983	Hammer	P. Dickinson	AAA	75.08
1987	Relay		AAA	40.75
1984	1600m relay		AAA	3 09.14

SELECT BIBLIOGRAPHY

Books and pamphlets
Buchanan I., Encyclopaedia of British Records (1961) & British Olympians (1991); *Ekkehard Z.M.*, Progression of World Best Performances (1987); *Greenall R.L.*, Leicester Newspapers 1851-1874 (1979); *Gwynn R.*, Guinness Book of the Marathon (1984); *Leicester City Council,* Saffron Lane Sports Centre (1967); *Lovesey P.*, Official Centenary History of the AAA (1979); *Mason A.*, Sport in Britain: a Social History (1992); *Matthews P.*, Guiness Book of Athletics Facts & Feats (1982); *Mitchell R.*, Midland Counties Athletic Association (1980); *Race Walking Association,* Sport of Race Walking (1962); *Simmons J.*, New University (1951); *Snow E.E.*, History of Leicestershire Cricket (1949); *Watman M.*, Encyclopaedias of Track & Field Events (five editions, 1964-81); *Webster F.A.M.*, Athletics of Today (1929); *Wright A.*, One Hundred Years of Midland Cross Country (1981).

Newspapers & periodicals
Athletics Weekly; Leicester Athlete & Midland Bicycle News; Leicester Chronicle & Mercury United; Leicester Evening Mail; Leicester Journal; Leicester Mercury; Leicester Sports Mercury; Loughborough Echo; Race Walking Record; The Times.

Other sources
Tozer M., "Physical Education at Thring's Uppingham" (unpublished thesis, University of Leicester, 1976); University of Birmingham, Centre of Athletics Literature.